WITHDRAWN

MAR 10 2004

CALLOWAY COUNTY PUBLIC LIBRARY
710 Main Street
MURRAY, KY 42071

FLORENCES'

GLASS KITCHEN

SHAKERS

1930 – 1950s

Identification & Value Guide

GENE &
CATHY
FLORENCE

COLLECTOR BOOKS
A Division of Schroeder Publishing Co., Inc.

D1277973

Front cover: Hazel-Atlas Windmills, $65.00 pair; McKee Hand-painted Lady, $65.00; McKee Jadite Badge Open, Flour and Sugar, $125.00 each, Salt and Pepper, $100.00 each; McKee Roman Arch Patriotic, $95.00 pair; and Tipp Novelty Company Cattails, Red, $24.00 each.

Back cover: Tipp Novelty Company Cherries, Set of eight on white trellis stand, $225.00; Tipp Novelty Company Cattails, Red, Large, Black Lids, Set of four on black stand, $125.00.

Cover design by Beth Summers
Book design by Terri Hunter

COLLECTOR BOOKS
P.O. Box 3009
Paducah, Kentucky 42002-3009
www.collectorbooks.com

Copyright © 2004 Gene and Cathy Florence

All rights reserved. No part of this book may be reproduced, stored in any retrieval system, or transmitted in any form, or by any means including but not limited to electronic, mechanical, photocopy, recording, or otherwise, without the written consent of the authors and publisher.

The current values in this book should be used only as a guide. They are not intended to set prices, which vary from one section of the country to another. Auction prices as well as dealer prices vary greatly and are affected by condition as well as demand. Neither the authors nor the publisher assumes responsibility for any losses that might be incurred as a result of consulting this guide.

Searching For A Publisher?

We are always looking for people knowledgeable within their fields. If you feel that there is a real need for a book on your collectible subject and have a large comprehensive collection, contact Collector Books.

Contents

Acknowledgments

There is little we can write that would adequately acknowledge the enthusiasm, time, and effort expended by Geri and Dan Tucker toward getting this book on shaker collecting before the public. They have personally traveled to the studio twice for photography sessions and that is no small feat as it entails organizing, wrapping, transporting, unwrapping, and rewrapping each shaker for travel. They have located shakers, shipped packages, and e-mailed photos over the entire period of "the hunt for shakers!" They have helped us identify, price, and proof. The catalog pages made available from Tipp City Novelty Company documenting pattern names belonged to them. What a find those pages were!

Collating photos from several of my earlier and current books became first a nightmare for me, and then Terri Hunter at Collector Books; but she did a fabulous job of design and layout with myriad parts and pieces. I also need to thank Amy Sullivan for typing my handwritten copy on hard-to-read plastic pages. Gail Ashburn, my editor, diligently went through my marked-up copy with Amy and reluctantly agreed it might work that way — and it did. Working with the helpful staff at Collector Books has been a pleasure with this logistically unfriendly book.

Collector Books' photographer, Charles Lynch, did most of the photography for this book and captured wonderful photos in one marathon and several quick photo shoots.

Additional help in pricing came from Lorrie Kitchen who specializes in kitchenware collectibles.

I appreciate my wife Cathy's work on this. Her hours on it equal mine — which were long!

SALT AND PEPPER

Silly little salt in your pretty pouring pitcher
Sitting benignly on my table making all my foods taste richer.

Do you know your history glorious, full of blood and guts and gore?
Did you hear of Carthage's anguish o'er those ruined fields of yore?

Did you truly form a pillared tomb for Lot's backward-looking wife?
And have you marched with every soldier behind the drum and fife?

I've heard you cauterized the wounds on battlefields of old
And that ancient peoples counted your wealth aside their gold.

You have known the convict's labor and the buffalo's touch
How came you in history's picture to mean so very much?

You were spoken of by Jesus as something having worth
For one so long important, why now this lowly berth?

Why sit you there upon my table so meek and unobtrusive?
You should shout and yell the heights your powers so inclusive.

How hold you such antitheses within your daily bill
To preserve or melt, corrode or clean, to cure — or, yes, to kill?

You've sat with queens and fed some kings, even delineated station as "Below!" for peasant crew —
An element necessary to life yet given thought by few.

Inward blackened pepper pot, well may you sit and stare
Who once was worth your weight in gold now my potato shares.

I've heard it said, though of its truth forsooth, I do not know
That first you crossed from east to west in chests of venturesome Polo.

How came you to those slant-eyed shores? Who found your flavor keys?
And who, I wonder, was first startled by that breath-defying sneeze?

Salt and pepper, black and white, a most deceptive pair
Who quietly, but surely bridge barriers — everywhere!

Cathy Florence (circa 1970s)

See pg. 139.

See pg. 139.

While photographing kitchen shakers for my *Florence's Big Book of Salt and Pepper Shakers,* Geri Tucker casually commented that she thought she had enough shakers available to her to create a book solely on kitchen and range shakers. Not one to let grass grow underfoot, I asked how serious she was about that and how many shakers she could get together! This book started from that "moment." Not every kitchen shaker known is included, of course, but representative examples of as many as we could find are here and many examples are shown due to Geri's and Dan's efforts.

Collecting range and kitchen shakers has increased dramatically since the advent of Internet listings and auctions. Before that, shakers had to be found in local shops, antique malls, and in a few nationally distributed collectors' newspapers. A collector had little recourse for buying shakers except in their limited surroundings. Now, a set of shakers in Florida or Australia is within their grasp with a few strokes on a computer. That has resulted in some spirited competition and intense price acceleration. There are now some large collections that could never have been gathered without the Internet.

See pg. 33.

This book is useful for those who know little about shakers as well as those who know more than we do. It is organized by company, shapes, and patterns; it is as structured as we could make it, and hopefully informal enough to be enjoyable. There is no one way to collect shakers. Gather those you like! If you like expensive ones, then you will not have as many, but quantity is not the goal of most collectors. They seek quality shakers in great condition. Shakers are practical for their original purposes and make wonderful decorations. Indeed, I've now seen them used as very imaginative décor in homes I've visited! They are not just found in kitchens anymore!

See pg. 33.

Range shakers are one category of many items for which Hocking is renowned. Notable are those made for use with their Fire-King patterns and Vitrock lines. These were often accompanied by grease jars, a few of which are included in the catalog pages presented.

Lithographed shaker tops' conditions are extremely important on shakers and this is reflected in higher shaker prices for those found in mint form. For mint condition prices, shakers have to have correct factory lids. For example, Apples (pg. 23) and Kitchen Aids (pg. 19) need white lids with a script S and P, and the Ivory shakers on page 23 should have a trio of tulip pots on their lids to be considered mint.

Assorted Fired-On

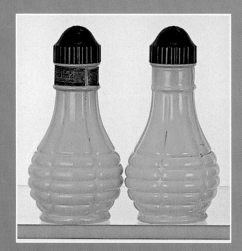

FIRED-ON Green
With label, $10.00
Without label, $9.00

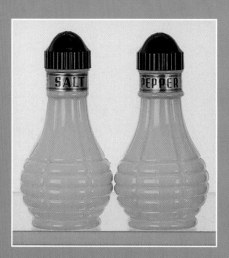

FIRED-ON Coral
With label, $10.00
Without label, $9.00

FIRED-ON Blue
With label, $10.00
Without label, $9.00

FIRED-ON
Dark Green,
$12.00

PHILCO
Boxed set, $40.00
Salt & pepper, $5.00 ea.
Mint salt tulip top, add $18.00
Mint pepper tulip top, add $12.00
Worn tops, add $2.00 – 3.00 only

PANELED, Black
  With label, $22.00
  Without label, $17.00

Slanted or Straight Letters
  Salt (not shown), $25.00
  Pepper, $22.00
  Salt & pepper, $50.00
  Flour, $45.00
  Sugar, $45.00
  Set of four, $150.00

PANELED, Blue
  Salt, pepper, flour, sugar
    With label, $22.00 ea.
    Without label, $18.00 ea.

LETTERED, Blue
  Salt, pepper, flour, sugar, $50.00 ea.
  Set of four, $210.00

Fired-On Green and Decorated

FIRED-ON Green Lettered
Salt, $40.00
Spice, $95.00
Sugar, $60.00
Flour, $60.00
Pepper, $40.00
Tea, $95.00

FIRED-ON Green Decorated
$65.00 ea.

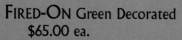

FIRED-ON Green Decorated
$75.00 ea.

FIRED-ON Yellow Lettered
    Salt, $45.00
    Pepper, $45.00
    Salt & pepper, $95.00
    Flour, $65.00
    Sugar, $65.00
    Set of four, $235.00

Green Clambroth and Yellow Opaque

GREEN CLAMBROTH Paneled, $50.00 ea.

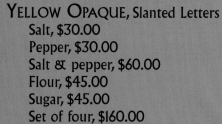

YELLOW OPAQUE, Slanted Letters
Salt, $30.00
Pepper, $30.00
Salt & pepper, $60.00
Flour, $45.00
Sugar, $45.00
Set of four, $160.00

Green Transparent

Paneled, $28.00 ea.
Domino labeled, $30.00
Round shakers, $40.00 ea.
Grease jar, $55.00
8 oz. square jars, $22.00 ea.
8 oz. round jars, $35.00 ea.

CALLOWAY COUNTY PUBLIC LIBRARY
710 Main Street
MURRAY, KY 42071

ALL PROVEN SELLERS

PANTRY, REFRIGERATOR AND MIXING BOWL SETS

A. G151—8-PCE. GREEN PANTRY SET
Set consists of
Four G526 Jars w/ Glass Covers
(Labelled Sugar, Flour, Cereal and Coffee)
Four G523 Jars, Aluminum Tops
(Labelled Spice, Sugar, Salt and Pepper)
1 Set in Carton, 10½ lbs.
Every housewife will appreciate this Set. It's one thing that will materially help to keep order in the pantry or kitchen. "A place for everything and everything in its place." Made of a delicate Green Glass with black and silver-colored labels, it adds color as well as convenience to any household. Order 25 or 50 sets, fill up your window with the cartons, make a mass display, show one set unpacked and you'll be surprised with its appeal.

B. G148—6-PCE. GREEN REFRIGERATOR SET
Set consists of one each
G31—6″ Oval Refrig. Jar & Cover
G33—7″ Oval Refrig. Jar & Cover
G35—8″ Oval Refrig. Jar & Cover
1 Set in Carton, 7 lbs.
A very necessary accessory to your Refrigerator. These money-saving covered Jars preserve food and conserve space. Just the thing for left-overs, salads, butter, sandwich fillings and other foods that must be kept for several days. All Jars have convenient recessed knobs in Covers. Jars can be stacked one upon the other if desired. These Sets can be most effectively used as sale-closers with Refrigerator purchasers. A set costs but little and accomplishes wonderful results for you.

C. G149—5-PCE. GREEN MIXING BOWL SET
Set consists of one each
6¼″ Green Glass Mixing Bowl
7¼″ Green Glass Mixing Bowl
8¼″ Green Glass Mixing Bowl
9¼″ Green Glass Mixing Bowl
10¼″ Green Glass Mixing Bowl
1 Set in Carton, 10 lbs.
These Green Mixing Bowls have rolled edge and self-balancing features. The Rolled Edge affords a convenient hand grip and prevents chipping. The bottom construction of these Bowls causes them, when tipped, to rest in a suitable position for mixing. They will not roll from side to side, as the ordinary Mixing Bowl does. The side panels aid in holding the Bowl and are quite decorative. These Bowls are highly polished and a delightful accessory to any kitchen.

Fired–On Red and Uitrock

FIRED-ON Red Paneled
Salt, pepper, flour, sugar
With label, $22.00 ea.
Without label, $18.00 ea.

FIRED-ON Red Lettered
Salt, $40.00
Pepper, $40.00
Salt & pepper, $82.50
Flour, $60.00
Sugar, $60.00
Set of four, $210.00

VITROCK
Salt, pepper, flour, sugar, spice, $35.00 ea.

Vitrock

BLACK CIRCLE
Salt, $30.00
Pepper, $30.00
Salt & pepper, $62.50
Flour, $35.00
Sugar, $35.00
Set of four, $135.00
Grease or range jar, $50.00

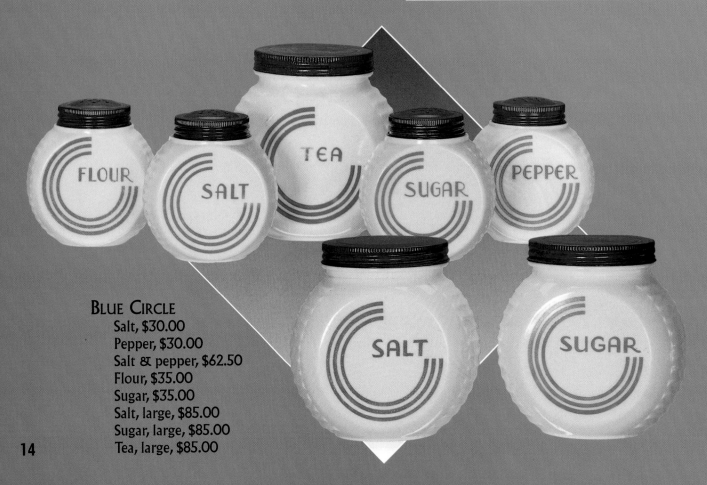

BLUE CIRCLE
Salt, $30.00
Pepper, $30.00
Salt & pepper, $62.50
Flour, $35.00
Sugar, $35.00
Salt, large, $85.00
Sugar, large, $85.00
Tea, large, $85.00

14

"VITROCK" KITCHEN BOWLS

W356—6" KITCHEN BOWL
Pkd. 4 doz. ctn.—wt. 42 lbs.

W357—7½" KITCHEN BOWL
Pkd. 2 doz. ctn.—wt. 35 lbs.

W359—9" KITCHEN BOWL
Pkd. 1 doz. ctn.—wt. 29 lbs.

W356—6" Dec. 404
Pkd. 4 doz. ctn.—wt. 42 lbs.

W357—7½" Dec. 404
Pkd. 2 doz. ctn.—wt. 35 lbs.

W359—9" Dec. 404
Pkd. 1 doz. ctn.—wt. 29 lbs.

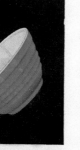  

W356—6" Dec. 1908
Pkd. 4 doz. ctn.—wt. 42 lbs.

W357—7½" Dec. 1908
Pkd. 2 doz. ctn.—wt. 35 lbs.

W359—9" Dec. 1908
Pkd. 1 doz. ctn.—wt. 29 lbs.

"VITROCK" RANGE JARS AND KITCHEN SHAKERS

W324—30 OZ. RANGE JAR &
COVER Dec. 4033
Pkd. 2 doz. ctn.—wt. 28 lbs.

W323—9 OZ. SALT SHAKER
Dec. 4033
Pkd. 2 doz. ctn.—wt. 11 lbs.

W323—9 OZ. PEPPER SHAKER
Dec. 4033
Pkd. 2 doz. ctn.—wt. 11 lbs.
Also furnish shakers lettered
"Sugar" and "Flour"

W324—30 OZ. RANGE JAR &
COVER—Dec. 4034
Pkd. 2 doz. ctn.—wt. 28 lbs.

W323—9 OZ. SALT SHAKER
Dec. 4034
Pkd. 2 doz. ctn.—wt. 11 lbs.

W323—9 OZ. PEPPER SHAKER
Dec. 4034
Pkd. 2 doz. ctn.—wt. 11 lbs.
Also furnish shakers lettered
"Sugar" and "Flour".

THE HOCKING GLASS COMPANY, LANCASTER, OHIO   23

Vitrock

VITROCK
Salt, $10.00
Pepper, $10.00
Grease or range jar, $25.00

GREEN CIRCLE
Salt, $65.00
Pepper, $65.00
Grease or range jar, $125.00

RED CIRCLE

Salt, $30.00   Set of four, $135.00
Pepper, $30.00   Salt, large, $85.00
Salt & pepper, $62.50   Grease or range jar, screw-on lid, $50.00
Flour, $35.00   Grease or range jar, glass lid, $50.00
Sugar, $35.00

GREEN FLOWER POTS

Salt, $30.00   Flour, $35.00
Pepper, $30.00   Sugar, $35.00
Salt & pepper, $62.50 Set of four, $135.00
                      Grease or range jar, $40.00

RED FLOWER POTS

Salt, $25.00   Flour, $35.00
Pepper, $25.00   Sugar, $35.00
Salt & pepper, $62.50 Set of four, $125.00
                      Grease or range jar, $35.00

Vitrock

RED TULIPS

Salt, $25.00   Flour, $35.00
Pepper, $25.00   Grease or range jar, $35.00
Sugar, $35.00   Set of four, $125.00

RED TULIPS

Salt, $25.00
Pepper, $25.00
Set on stand, $65.00

IVORY KITCHENWARE

W323/4995—9 OZ. SALT
SHAKER
Pkd. 2 doz.—11 lbs.

W323/4995—9 OZ. PEPPER
SHAKER
Pkd. 2 doz.—11 lbs.

W324/4995—30 OZ. RANGE
JAR & COVER
Pkd. 2 doz.—28 lbs.

W786/2456—5¼" KITCHEN
BOWL—Red Bands
Pkd. 2 doz.—14 lbs.

W706/2456—6" KITCHEN
BOWL—Red Bands
Pkd. 2 doz.—24 lbs.

W707/2456—7½" KITCHEN
BOWL—Red Bands
Pkd. 2 doz.—34 lbs.

W709/2456—9" KITCHEN
BOWL—Red Bands
Pkd. 1 doz.—29 lbs.

ANCHOR HOCKING GLASS CORPORATION, LANCASTER, OHIO, U. S. A.

KITCHEN AIDS
Salt, $100.00
Pepper, $100.00
Salt & pepper, $210.00
Grease jar, $175.00
Set, $400.00
Set in box, $525.00

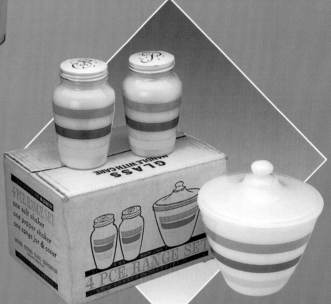

STRIPES
Salt, $25.00
Pepper, $25.00
Salt & pepper, $52.50
Grease jar, $65.00
Set, $125.00
Set in box, $195.00

RED DOTS
Salt, $25.00
Pepper, $25.00
Salt & pepper, $52.50
Grease jar, $55.00
Set, $115.00
Set in box, $185.00

Range Shakers

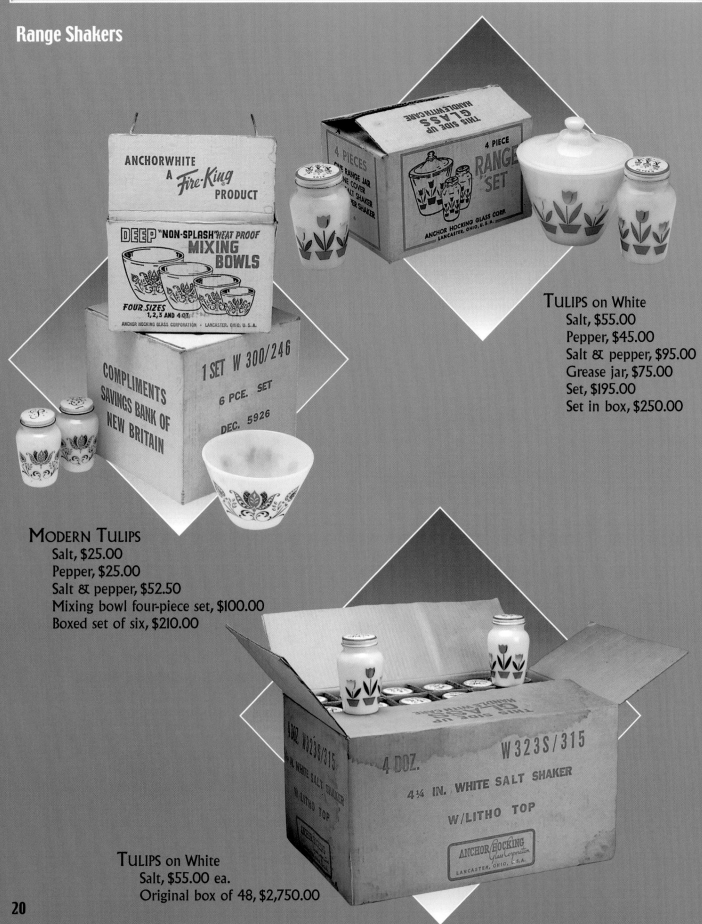

TULIPS on White
Salt, $55.00
Pepper, $45.00
Salt & pepper, $95.00
Grease jar, $75.00
Set, $195.00
Set in box, $250.00

MODERN TULIPS
Salt, $25.00
Pepper, $25.00
Salt & pepper, $52.50
Mixing bowl four-piece set, $100.00
Boxed set of six, $210.00

TULIPS on White
Salt, $55.00 ea.
Original box of 48, $2,750.00

MIXING BOWLS

PACKING

W4100/5 —4 Pce. Mixing Bowl Set .... 6 sets — 41 lbs.
    (Each Set in Gift Carton)

W4100/55—4 Pce. Mixing Bowl Set .... 2 doz. —150 lbs.
    (Bulk Packed in 6 Cartons)   sets

W4100/67—4 Pce. Mixing Bowl Set .... 8 sets — 48 lbs.
    (Each Set Nested & Packed in an Individual Cell)

The Sets listed above consist of one each of the
W4156, W4157, W4158 and W4159 Bowls

OPEN STOCK

W4156—6" Mixing Bowl	2 doz. —	19 lbs.
W4157—7" Mixing Bowl	2 doz. —	29 lbs.
W4158—8" Mixing Bowl	1 doz. —	22 lbs.
W4159—9" Mixing Bowl	1 doz. —	29 lbs.

PACKING

W300/130—3 Pce. Mixing Bowl Set .... 2 doz. — 66 lbs.
    (Bulk Packed in 3 Cartons)   sets
COMPOSITION: One each 4⅞", 6" and 7¼" Bowls

OPEN STOCK

W355—4⅞" Mixing Bowl	2 doz. —	13 lbs.
W356—6" Mixing Bowl	2 doz. —	20 lbs.
W357—7¼" Mixing Bowl	2 doz. —	33 lbs.
W358—8⅜" Mixing Bowl (Not Illustrated)	1 doz. —	27 lbs.

"KITCHEN AIDS" DECORATION

RANGE SET

W300/239—4 Pce. Range Set
    Each Set in Gift Carton, 8 Sets to Shipping Carton — 19 lbs.
COMPOSITION: One Salt Shaker—White Top
            One Pepper Shaker—White Top
            One Range Jar & Cover

The above Range Set and matching Mixing Bowl
Sets in "Kitchen Aids" decoration, are not
available in Open Stock.

W300/237—3 Pce. Mixing Bowl Set
    Each Set Nested & Packed in an Individual Cell,
    8 Sets to Shipping Carton — 44 lbs.
COMPOSITION: One 1 Qt. Mixing Bowl
            One 2 Qt. Mixing Bowl
            One 3 Qt. Mixing Bowl

W300/238—4 Pce. Mixing Bowl Set
    Each Set in Gift Carton, 4 Sets to Shipping Carton — 37 lbs.
COMPOSITION: One 1 Qt. Mixing Bowl
             One 2 Qt. Mixing Bowl
            One 3 Qt. Mixing Bowl
            One 4 Qt. Mixing Bowl

HEAT-PROOF

Anchorglass, 1959 – 1960 catalog, page 59

★ W23S   ★ W24   ★ W23P

★ W355   ★ W356   ★ W357

★ G23S   ★ G24   ★ G23P

★ G355   ★ G356   ★ G357

22

DESCRIPTION

*Fire-King**

IVORY

★ **W23S**—4¼" SALT SHAKER—
"LITHO" TOPS
Pkd. 4 doz.—wt. 18 lbs.
★ **W23P**—4¼" PEPPER SHAKER—
"LITHO" TOPS
Pkd. 4 doz.—wt. 18 lbs.
★ **W24** —16 OZ. CANISTER—"LITHO" TOP
Pkd. 4 doz.—wt. 32 lbs.
★ **W355**—4⅞" MIXING BOWL
Pkd. 3 doz.—wt. 19 lbs.
★ **W356**—6" MIXING BOWL
Pkd. 3 doz.—wt. 34 lbs.
★ **W357**—7¼" MIXING BOWL
Pkd. 3 doz.—wt. 55 lbs.

SETS

★ **W300/130**—3 PCE. MIXING BOWL SET
3 Doz. Sets Pkd. Bulk in
3 Ctns.—wt. 108 lbs.
COMPOSITION:
1 Ctn. W355 Mixing Bowl
1 Ctn. W356 Mixing Bowl
1 Ctn. W357 Mixing Bowl
★ **W300/132**—6 PCE. KITCHEN SET
Each Set Pkd. in Ind.
R/S Ctn.—wt. 5 lbs.
COMPOSITION:
One W355 Mixing Bowl
One W356 Mixing Bowl
One W357 Mixing Bowl
One W23S Salt Shaker—"Litho" Top
One W23P Pepper Shaker—"Litho" Top
One W24 Canister—"Litho" top

JADE-ITE

★ **G23S**—4¼" SALT SHAKER—
"LITHO" TOPS
Pkd. 4 doz.—wt. 18 lbs.
★ **G23P**—4¼" PEPPER SHAKER—
"LITHO" TOPS
Pkd. 4 doz.—wt. 18 lbs.
★ **G24** —16 OZ. CANISTER—"LITHO" TOPS
Pkd. 4 doz.—wt. 32 lbs.
★ **G355**—4⅞" MIXING BOWL
Pkd. 3 doz.—wt. 19 lbs.
★ **G356**—6" MIXING BOWL
Pkd. 3 doz.—wt. 34 lbs.
★ **G357**—7¼" MIXING BOWL
Pkd. 3 doz.—wt. 55 lbs.

SETS

★ **G300/129**—3 PCE. MIXING BOWL SET
3 Doz. Sets Pkd. Bulk in
3 Ctns.—wt. 108 lbs.
COMPOSITION:
1 Ctn. G355 Mixing Bowl
1 Ctn. G356 Mixing Bowl
1 Ctn. G357 Mixing Bowl
★ **G300/131**—6 PCE. KITCHEN SET
Each Set Pkd. in Ind.
R/S Ctn.—wt. 5 lbs.
COMPOSITION:
One G355 Mixing Bowl
One G356 Mixing Bowl
One G357 Mixing Bowl
One G23S Salt Shaker—"Litho" Top
One G23P Pepper Shaker—"Litho" Top
One G24 Canister—"Litho" Top

*Reg. U. S. Pat. Off.

IVORY with Tulip Tops
Salt, $25.00
Pepper, $18.00
Salt & pepper, $45.00
With "S" top, $10.00
With "P" top, $7.00
Pair of "S" & "P" tops, $18.00

BLACK DOTS
Salt, $35.00
Pepper, $32.00
Salt & pepper, $70.00

JADE-ITE with Tulip Tops
Salt, $65.00
Pepper, $58.00
Salt & pepper, $125.00

PRIMROSE, $195.00

APPLE, Salt, $35.00

Bartlett Collins Glass Company

Bartlett-Collins produced several collectible shaker designs. The Kitchen Chef shakers pictured are decorated to match Hazel-Atlas mugs and Federal glass plates, making an interesting assortment of similar designed wares from several glass companies. The Kitchen Chef decoration has also been found on Anchor Hocking range shakers like those pictured on page 23. There were 16-oz. and 32-oz. jars produced to match some of the other shakers shown. The 16-oz. jar was marketed as a grease jar and the 32-oz. as a cookie jar.

Chefs and Dutch

KITCHEN CHEF, 3¾"
Salt, $30.00
Pepper, $30.00
Salt & pepper, $65.00

PURPLE GRAPE, $12.00 ea.

DUTCH
Salt, $16.00
Pepper, $16.00
32 oz. cookie jar, $40.00
16 oz. grease jar, $40.00

Fenton shakers are not as prevalent as those of other companies, but their Emerald Glo shakers are found in many collections with or without Star cuttings. Tops were either gold or silver colored, depending upon accoutrements included as parts of larger sets. The Hobnail shaker pictured can also be found in white.

EMERALD GLO
Salt & pepper, $25.00
With label, $15.00 ea.

HOBNAIL #3602, black, $30.00

Gemco Products

Shakers from Gemco are collected for their vivid and bright colors, although they were also manufactured in crystal. Tops for the shakers are often found in excellent shape. Prices for these shakers are generally easier on the pocketbook than many of the other shakers in this book.

FIRED-ON, $10.00

6-pc. set on revolving tray, $50.00

Tall yellow, $12.00

Kitchen shakers made by Hazel-Atlas are desired for their numerous designs. Hazel-Atlas range shakers are found in two basic shapes, round with ribs and square. We have divided each of these shapes into patterns using known designations from collectors. In some cases, no consistent names have been forthcoming; so we have simply presented a terminology in order for collectors to know what particular shakers are being discussed in ads or auctions.

Most designs were established by Hazel-Atlas but some were designated by decorating firms Gay Fad and Tipp Novelty Company. Many Hazel-Atlas shakers are marked with the familiar "H" over "A" on the bottom, but some are not.

Confusion still exists between the square shakers of McKee and those of Hazel-Atlas. Hazel-Atlas square shakers have a distinct sharp edge down the corners whereas McKee shakers have less sharp, more rounded edges. The screw threads on top of Hazel-Atlas shakers are immediately on top of the squared design, but McKee shakers have a rounded shoulder before the threads are encountered. This should help distinguish between the two if the shakers are not marked.

ROOSTERS

Salt, $22.00   Flour, $25.00
Pepper, $22.00   Sugar, $25.00
Salt & pepper, $45.00 Set of four, $100.00

"STARS"
Salt, $22.00
Pepper, $22.00
Salt & pepper, $48.00
Double price for mint condition.

ARROWS, blue or red
Salt, $35.00
Pepper, $20.00

FIRED-ON
Salt, green, $30.00
Pepper, pastel green, $35.00
Flour, yellow, $35.00
Salt, pink, $35.00
Pepper, green, $30.00

Round Ribbed

FIRED-ON Red

Salt, $30.00   Flour, $30.00
Pepper, $30.00   Sugar, $30.00
Salt & pepper, $65.00   Set of four, $130.00

OLD ENGLISH, Decorated Red   **BOLD STRIPE,** Decorated Red
Salt, $32.00   Salt, $32.00
Pepper, $30.00   Pepper, $30.00
Salt & pepper, $65.00   Salt & pepper, $65.00

GREEN STRIPES

Salt, $25.00	Flour, $33.00
Pepper, $20.00	Sugar, $33.00
Salt & pepper, $48.00	Set of four, $120.00

RED STRIPES

Salt, $25.00

Pepper, $20.00

Flour, $33.00

Sugar, $33.00

Set of four, $120.00

Round Ribbed Platonite

BLACK LETTERS

Salt, $18.00   Flour, $24.00
Pepper, $18.00   Sugar, $24.00
Salt & pepper, $40.00   Set of four, $90.00

COLONIAL COUPLE, $35.00

RED/YELLOW STRIPE

Salt, $35.00   Flour, $35.00
Pepper, $35.00   Sugar, $35.00
Salt & pepper, $75.00   Set of four, $150.00

SCRIPTED LETTERS, Large
Salt, $22.00
Pepper, $22.00
Salt & pepper, $45.00
Flour, $25.00
Sugar, $25.00
Set of four, $100.00

SCRIPTED LETTERS, Small
Pepper, $16.00
Spices:
Cinnamon, $18.00
Nutmeg, $18.00
Celery salt, $18.00
Ginger, $18.00
Cloves, $18.00
Paprika, $18.00

Square

DECO

Salt, $65.00	Flour, $65.00
Pepper, $65.00	Sugar, $65.00
Salt & pepper, $135.00	Set of four, $275.00

ELECTROCHET or EMBOSSED HOT POINT

Salt, $20.00	Flour, $26.00
Pepper, $20.00	Sugar, $26.00
Salt & pepper, $42.00	Set of four, $100.00

DUTCH Fired-On Colors

Large, 4½"
  Salt, $30.00
  Pepper, $30.00
  Salt & pepper, $65.00
  Flour, $32.00
  Sugar, $32.00
  Set of four, $135.00

Small on stand, 3⅛"
  Salt, $15.00
  Pepper, $15.00
  Salt & pepper, $32.00
  Flour, $18.00
  Sugar, $18.00
  Set of four, $70.00
  Set of four on stand, $85.00

Small narrow, 3⅜"
  Salt, $18.00
  Pepper (not shown), $18.00
  Salt & pepper, $38.00
  Flour, $20.00
  Sugar (not shown), $28.00
  Set of four, $85.00

Hazel-Atlas Glass Company

Square

DUTCH, Large, 4½"
Salt, $25.00
Pepper, $25.00
Salt & pepper, $55.00

DUTCH, Small, 3⅛"
Salt, $20.00
Pepper, $20.00
Salt & pepper, $45.00

DUTCH, Small narrow, 3⅜"
Salt, $20.00
Pepper, $20.00
Salt & pepper, $45.00
With stand, $60.00

DUTCH SKATERS, Red
  Salt, $30.00
  Pepper, $30.00
  Salt & pepper, $65.00
  Flour, $35.00
  Sugar, $35.00
  Set of four, $140.00

DUTCH SKATERS, Green or Blue
  Salt, green, $30.00
  Pepper, green, $30.00
  Salt & pepper, green, $65.00
  Flour, blue, $35.00
  Sugar, blue, $35.00
  Set of four, $140.00

Square

0-3874/3117—4 oz. Dec.
Range Shaker
Pkd. 4 doz. ctn. Wt. 17 lbs.
Height 3³/₁₆"

0-3874/3118—4 oz. Dec.
Range Shaker
Pkd. 4 doz. ctn. Wt. 17 lbs.
Height 3³/₁₆"

Glassware by Hazel-Atlas,
1957 catalog, page 31

WINDMILLS, large, 4½"
    Salt, $30.00
    Pepper, $30.00
    Salt & pepper, $65.00

WINDMILLS, small, 3⅛"
    Salt (not shown), $22.00
    Pepper, $22.00
    Salt & pepper, $45.00

DUTCH, 3⅜"
    Salt, $20.00
    Pepper, $20.00
    Salt & pepper, $45.00
    Flour, $25.00
    Sugar, $25.00
    Set of four, $110.00
    Set of four on stand, $125.00

Square

DUTCH TULIPS by Gay Fad

Large Yellow
  Salt, $40.00
  Sugar, $40.00
  Allspice, $40.00
  Cloves, $40.00
  Oil, $40.00

Large Red
  Pepper, $45.00
  Cinnamon, $45.00
  Nutmeg, $45.00

Small Red
  Pepper, $40.00

EMBOSSED Transparent, Pink
  Salt, $60.00
  Pepper, $60.00
  Salt & pepper, $125.00

EMBOSSED Transparent, Crystal
  Salt (not shown), $30.00
  Pepper, $30.00
  Salt & pepper, $65.00

EMBOSSED Transparent, Green
  Salt, $60.00
  Pepper, $60.00
  Salt & pepper, $125.00
  Flour, $90.00
  Sugar, $90.00
  Set of four, $325.00

Square

SQUARE BLOCK, Fleur de Lis
  Small, 8 oz.
      Salt (not shown), $14.00
      Pepper, $14.00
      Salt & pepper, $30.00

  Medium, 16 oz.
      Salt, $18.00
      Pepper (not shown), $18.00
      Salt & pepper, $40.00

  Large, 20 oz.
      Flour, $35.00
      Sugar, $35.00

BLOCK DESIGN
  Block Letter Spices, $16.00 ea.

BLOCK DESIGN, Plain (no lettering)

Had label with food product
Example: Embassy Peanut Butter, 8 oz., shown.
  Small, $5.00; with label, $15.00
  Large, $15.00; with label, $25.00

IVY, Green
    Salt, $60.00
    Pepper, $60.00
    Salt & pepper, $125.00

IVY, Dark Green
    Salt (not shown), $60.00
    Pepper, $60.00
    Salt & pepper, $125.00

PENNSYLVANIA DUTCH SYMBOL
    Salt, $25.00
    Pepper, $25.00
    Salt & pepper, $50.00
    Roastmeat Seasoning, two styles, $30.00 ea.

Square

SHIELD, Black

Salt, $18.00   Flour, $22.00
Pepper, $18.00   Sugar, $22.00
Salt & pepper, $38.00   Set of four, $85.00

SHIELD, Green
Salt, $18.00
Pepper, $18.00
Salt & pepper, $38.00

SHIELD WITH DOTS, Blue

Salt, $60.00   Flour, $95.00
Pepper, $60.00   Sugar, $95.00
Salt & pepper, $125.00   Set of four, $325.00

SHIELD WITH DOTS, Red

Salt, $60.00   Flour, $95.00
Pepper, $60.00   Sugar, $95.00
Salt & pepper, $125.00   Set of four, $325.00

Square

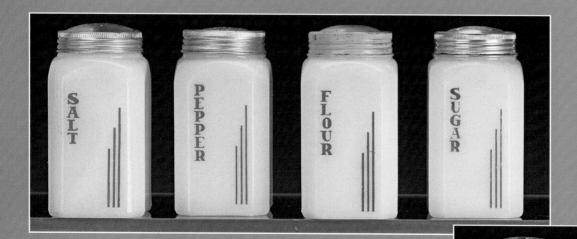

VERTICAL LINES, Black or Red
    Salt, $30.00
    Pepper, $30.00
    Salt & pepper, $65.00
    Flour, $40.00
    Sugar, $40.00
    Set of four, $150.00

VERTICAL LINES, Green
    Salt, $35.00
    Pepper, $35.00
    Salt & pepper, $75.00

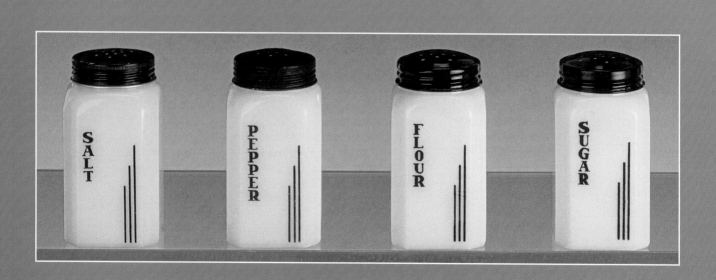

FIRED-ON Black
Salt, $25.00

FIRED-ON Yellow
Pepper, $25.00

FIRED-ON "Beige" Flour (not shown), $25.00

FIRED-ON Green
Sugar, $25.00
Set of four, $110.00

FIRED-ON Black
Salt, $25.00
Pepper, $25.00
Salt & pepper, $55.00

VERTICAL RIBBED, Round
    Blue, $12.00 ea., $25.00 pr.
    Crystal, $5.00 ea., $10.00 pr.
    Green, $10.00 ea., $22.00 pr.
    Red, $10.00 ea., $22.00 pr.
    Yellow, $12.00 ea., $26.00 pr.

VERTICAL RIBBED, Tall
    Green, $10.00 ea., $22.00 pr.
    Yellow, $10.00 ea., $22.00 pr.

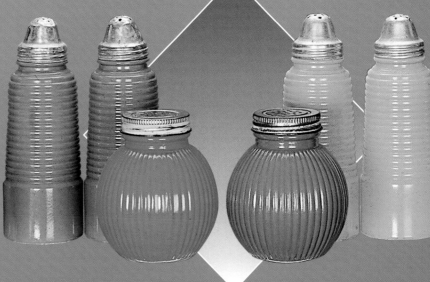

Hazel-Atlas Glass Company

Miscellaneous

Restaurant and Institutional Ware by **HAZEL-ATLAS**

477-8—1 oz. Salt & Pepper Shaker—Nickel Pltd. Brass Tops Pkd. 6 doz. ctn. Wt. 13 lbs. Height 3⁵⁄₁₆" Top ⅞"

30—1⅝ oz. Salt & Pepper Shaker—Aluminum Tops Pkd. 6 doz. ctn. Wt. 14 lbs. Height 3³⁄₃₂" Top 1¼"

1533—¾ oz. Salt & Pepper Shaker—Nickel Pltd. Brass Tops Pkd. 6 doz. ctn. Wt. 9 lbs. Height 2²⁹⁄₃₂" Top ¾"

1038—2¾ oz. Barrel Salt and Pepper Shaker—Tin Tops, Red Coated Pkd. 6 doz. ctn. Wt. 15 lbs. Height 3" Top 2"

477-4—1 oz. Salt & Pepper Shaker—Stainless Steel Caps Pkd. 6 doz. ctn. Wt. 13 lbs. Height 3⅛" Top ⅞"

2442—2 oz. Salt & Pepper Shaker—Stainless Steel Caps Pkd. 6 doz. ctn. Wt. 19 lbs. Height 3½" Top 1⁵⁄₃₂"

4231—3 oz. Salt & Pepper Shaker—Stainless Steel Caps Pkd. 6 doz. ctn. Wt. 27 lbs. Height 4⅜" Top 1⁵⁄₃₂"

5053—4 oz. Salt & Pepper Shaker—Stainless Steel Caps Pkd. 2 doz. ctn. Wt. 8 lbs. Height 3¹⁹⁄₃₂" Top 1¾"

5053-410—4 oz. Sugar Server Stainless Steel Cap Self-closing spout Pkd. 2 doz. ctn. Wt. 9 lbs. Height 3¹⁹⁄₃₂" Top 1¾"

5053-710—4 oz. Cream Server (Ketchup or Mustard Server) Stainless Steel Cap Pkd. 2 doz. ctn. Wt. 9 lbs. Height 3¹⁹⁄₃₂" Top 1¾"

5052-970—12 oz. Sugar Server Stainless Steel Cap Center hole Pkd. 2 doz. ctn. Wt. 20 lbs. Height 5¾" Top 2⅜"

5052-920—12 oz. Sugar Server Stainless Steel Cap Self-closing spout Pkd. 2 doz. ctn. Wt. 20 lbs. Height 5¾" Top 2⅜"

†Item numbers within ( ) in light face type are the former numbers

21

477-7—1 oz. Salt & Pepper Shaker—Molded Tops—Red Pkd. 6 doz. ctn. Wt. 12 lbs. Height 3⁷⁄₁₆" Top ⅞"

Glassware by Hazel–Atlas, 1957 catalog, page 21

Astor Pure Nutmeg, $12.50

Current reproduction, Green

44

BUTTER CHURNING LADIES
Salt, $25.00
Pepper, $25.00
Pair with stand, $65.00

SMALL
Crystal, $6.00
Green, $10.00
Pink (not shown), $10.00

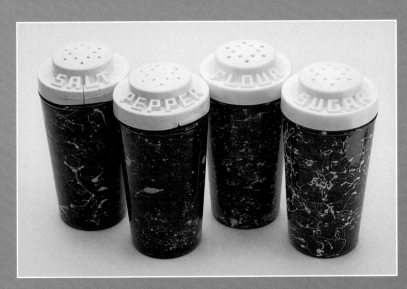

SPATTERWARE, Black, attributed to Hazel-Atlas but unmarked, $15.00 ea.

SPATTERWARE, Red
Salt, $35.00
Pepper, $35.00
Salt & pepper, $75.00
Flour, $45.00
Sugar, $49.00
Set of four, $165.00

Jeannette Glass Company

Jennyware, and the much in demand, rounded, opaque shakers are the most familiar Jeannette shakers to collectors. Note the advertisements pictured on page 47 which show that both flat and footed Jennyware shakers were used with the small Jennyware mixing bowl as a grease set! Grease jars are most often found with covers, but this shows that not all grease sets had lids. Rounded jadite shakers were often used for both kitchen and bath products; thus some toiletry items have been included in this section, and they are extremely desirable to advanced collectors.

Jennyware Footed Shakers

Crystal
Salt, $20.00
Pepper, $20.00
Salt & pepper, $45.00
Without labels, $15.00 ea.

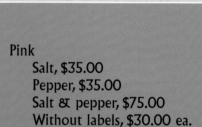

Pink
Salt, $35.00
Pepper, $35.00
Salt & pepper, $75.00
Without labels, $30.00 ea.

Ultramarine
Salt, $35.00
Pepper, $35.00
Salt & pepper, $75.00
Without labels, $30.00 ea.

Round, Crystal
Salt, $30.00
Pepper, $30.00
Salt & pepper, $65.00
Without labels, $22.00 ea.

Flat, Pink
Salt, $45.00
Pepper, $45.00
Salt & pepper, $95.00
Without labels, $38.00 ea.

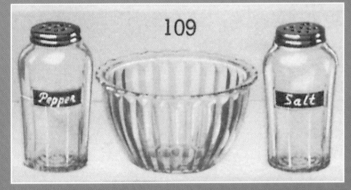

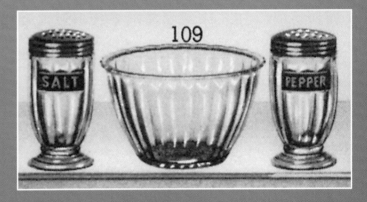

Comparison of Jennyware shakers
Page 4 of 1939 (above) and 1940 (right)
Gold Cross Milk Premiums & Recipes

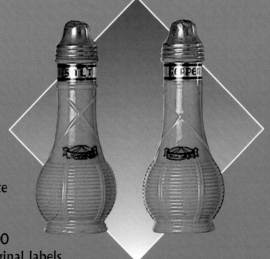

BASKETWEAVE, Delphite
Salt, $15.00
Pepper, $15.00
Salt & pepper, $35.00
*Add $3.00 for original labels

Jeannette Glass Company

Delphite

Square
   Salt, $80.00
   Pepper, $80.00
   Salt & pepper, $165.00
   Flour, $100.00
   Sugar, $100.00
   Set of four, $275.00

Round
   Salt, $50.00
   Pepper, $50.00
   Salt & pepper, $105.00
   Flour (not shown), $75.00
   Sugar, $75.00
   Set of four, $260.00
   Paprika, $100.00

The word "Jadite" was used by most companies, including Jeannette and McKee, to describe their opaque green color. Jade-ite (with the hyphen) was used only by Anchor Hocking for their opaque green beginning in 1945 with their introduction of what collectors now call "Jane Ray."

Original tops on spices such as red pepper shown are pewter painted black.

Kitchen Shakers, Round

Salt, $30.00   Flour, $60.00
Pepper, $30.00   Sugar, $60.00
Salt & pepper, $65.00 Set of four, $190.00
                      Red pepper (mint lid), $75.00
                      *Add $5.00 for decoration

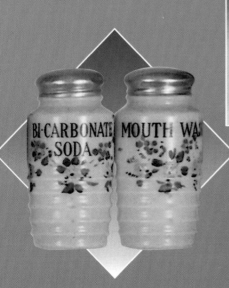

Bath Shakers, Round, usually with black plastic or wood tops.
    Decorated, $125.00 ea.
    Non-decorated, $110.00 ea.

Jadite

Jadite Light, Square

Dark is rarer but light has more demand, so prices are the same for both.

Salt, $70.00
Pepper, $70.00
Salt & pepper, $145.00
Flour, $85.00
Sugar, $85.00
Set of four, $325.00

Jadite Dark, Square

McKee had two distinct range shaker shapes. Collectors have decreed the first style (pages 51 – 63) as "Roman Arches." The remaining McKee shakers shown represent the square style (with the more rounded edges). See page 26 for an explanation of how to distinguish McKee's square shakers from those of Hazel-Atlas. We have used factory names when known and collectors' designations when possible in order to keep "names" recognizable to the collecting community. Original names have been used in place of accepted terms in some cases, but only with documentation.

Numerous McKee shakers were decorated by the factory, but many were sold to be decorated by someone else. Most notable were those adorned by Tipp (Tippecanoe) City Decorating Company. In the Tipp Novelty Company section, we show actual catalog pages of Tipp's patterns on McKee shakers. See page 87 for a more detailed explanation of these decorations.

Notice that there are some McKee shakers fetching serious prices. Those are rarely found today, but there are some sophisticated collectors searching for them. As with any collectible in short supply, there have to be more collectors willing to pay the price than there is supply. There are rarely seen shakers which do not fetch exorbitant prices, because only a few collectors want them. (Demand is more important than supply when it comes to pricing.)

Jadite and Delphite have always been collected, but some of the designs on these colors are suddenly more popular than in the past. Color is important, but finding mint condition designs on those colors adds to the value of sought items.

Roman Arch

Mostly found in Canada and sometimes found with granite ware tray that fits on back of stove.

Salt, $60.00
Pepper, $60.00
Salt & pepper, $125.00
Flour, $95.00
Sugar, $95.00
Set of four, $315.00

Roman Arch

FRENCH CANADIAN
Custard with red (rare), $110.00 ea.
White, short, black tops, $65.00 ea.
White, tall, metal tops, $80.00 ea.

Bow Tie
Salt, $60.00
Pepper, $60.00
Salt & pepper, $125.00
Flour (not shown), $95.00
Sugar (not shown), $95.00
Set of four, $325.00

Diamond Check
Salt (red), $95.00
Pepper (black), $95.00
Salt & pepper, $210.00
Flour (black) (not shown), $110.00
Sugar (red), $110.00
Set of four, $425.00

Roman Arch

DOTS, Green Script on Custard

Salt, $75.00	Flour, $95.00
Pepper, $75.00	Sugar, $95.00
Salt & pepper, $165.00	Set of four, $365.00

DOTS, Blue Script on Custard
Salt, $110.00
Pepper, $110.00
Salt & pepper, $225.00

DOTS, Red Script on White
    Flour, $110.00
    Sugar (not shown), $110.00
    Salt (not shown), $95.00
    Pepper (not shown), $95.00
    Set of four, $425.00

DOTS, Red on White with Initials
    Salt, $40.00
    Pepper, $40.00
    Salt & pepper, $85.00

DOTS, Red Script on Custard
Salt, $95.00	Flour, $110.00
Pepper, $95.00	Sugar, $110.00
Salt & pepper, $210.00	Set of four, $425.00

Roman Arch

Assorted Fired-On, Large, 3⅞"h x 2⅜"w,
White or Black Lettering
Salt, $40.00
Pepper, $40.00
Salt & pepper, $85.00
Flour, $40.00
Sugar, $75.00
Set of four, $210.00

Assorted Fired-On, Large, 3⅞"h x 2⅜"w

Salt, $40.00	Flour, $40.00
Pepper, $40.00	Sugar, $75.00
Salt & pepper, $85.00	Set of four, $210.00

Assorted Fired-On, Small, 3⁵⁄₁₆"h x 2³⁄₁₆"w

Salt, $40.00
*Pepper, $40.00
Salt & pepper, $85.00
Flour, $40.00
Sugar, $75.00
Set of four, $210.00

*Yellow pepper, $65.00

DeLuxe
KITCHENWARE
MADE BY
McKEE GLASS CO.
JEANNETTE, PA.
EST. 1853

Roman Arch

SCRIPT INITIALS, Custard
Salt, $30.00
Pepper, $30.00
Salt & pepper, $65.00

SCRIPT INITIALS, White
Salt, $25.00
Pepper, $25.00
Salt & pepper, $55.00

SCRIPT INITIALS or BLOCK, Black
Salt, $30.00
Pepper, $30.00
Salt & pepper, $65.00

Fired-On Red
  Salt, $25.00
  Pepper, $25.00
  Salt & pepper, $55.00
  Flour, $30.00
  Sugar, $30.00
  Set of four, $125.00

PATRIOTIC, God Bless America
  Salt, $45.00
  Pepper, $45.00
  Salt & pepper, $95.00

PATRIOTIC, Abraham Lincoln
  Salt with top, $35.00
  Pepper with top, $35.00
  ½ lb. butter, $95.00

Roman Arch

SCRIPT WORDS, Black, Large, 3⅞", with white letters
Salt, $25.00
Pepper, $25.00
Salt & pepper, $55.00
Flour, $30.00
Sugar, $30.00
Set of four, $120.00

SCRIPT WORDS, Black, Small, 3⁵⁄₁₆"
Salt, $30.00
Pepper, $30.00
Salt & pepper, $65.00
Flour, $35.00
Sugar, $35.00
Set of four, $140.00

SCRIPT WORDS, Black, Large, 3⅞", with red letters
Salt, $35.00
Pepper (not shown), $35.00
Salt & pepper, $75.00

SCRIPT WORDS, Crystal Frosted
Salt, $15.00
Pepper, $15.00
Salt & pepper, $32.00

SCRIPT WORDS, Custard, Black Letters
Salt, $20.00
Pepper, $20.00
Salt & pepper, $45.00
Flour, $35.00
Sugar, $35.00
Set of four, $120.00

SCRIPT WORDS, Custard, Red Letters
Flour, $45.00
Sugar, $45.00

SCRIPT WORDS, White, Black Letters

Salt, $18.00	Flour, $20.00
Pepper, $18.00	Sugar, $20.00
Salt & pepper, $40.00	Set of four, $85.00

Roman Arch

SCRIPT WORDS, Jadite
Salt, $110.00
Pepper, $110.00
Salt & pepper, $225.00
Flour, $175.00
Sugar, $175.00
Set of four, $600.00
Spice, $195.00
Cinnamon, $275.00

SCRIPT WORDS, Delphite
Salt, $175.00
Pepper, $175.00
Salt & pepper, $365.00

SHIPS, Black
  Salt, $65.00
  Pepper, $65.00
  Salt & pepper, $135.00

SHIPS, Red, Small, Red Tops
  Salt, $25.00
  Pepper, $25.00
  Salt & pepper, $55.00
  Flour, $35.00
  Sugar, $35.00
  Set of four, $130.00

SHIPS, Red, Large
  Sugar, $40.00
  Flour, $40.00

Advertising, Roman Arch, and Square

Square shakers are divided into sections of McKee decorated (pages 64 – 86) and those decorated by Tipp Novelty Company (beginning on page 87). Most McKee shakers are desirable no matter who their decorator.

SHERATON
Salt, $100.00
Pepper, $100.00
Salt & pepper, $225.00

BATCHELOR BROS.
Salt, $100.00
Pepper, $100.00
Salt & pepper, $225.00

CHEF'S HEAD
Flour, $125.00
Sugar, $125.00

POMCO
Salt, $60.00
Pepper, $60.00
Salt & pepper, $125.00

Square

White, CHEF BOYARDEE
on bottom
Salt, $25.00
Pepper, $25.00
Salt & pepper, $55.00
Flour, $25.00
Sugar, $25.00
Set of four, $110.00

TAPPAN
Salt, $10.00
Pepper, $10.00
Salt & pepper, $22.00

HUETHER'S BEER,
$275.00

Jeannette Glass
50th Anniversary, $750.00 pr.

Square

APRON LADY, Custard
    Salt (not shown), $105.00
    Pepper, $105.00
    Salt & pepper, $220.00
    Flour (not shown), $135.00
    Sugar, $135.00
    Set of four, $500.00

APRON LADY, White
    Salt, $95.00
    Pepper, $95.00
    Salt & pepper, $195.00
    Flour, $125.00
    Sugar, $125.00
    Set of four, $400.00

DECO BADGE, Caramel
Flour, $95.00
Sugar, $95.00

BADGE, Custard
Salt, $75.00
Pepper, $75.00
Salt & pepper, $155.00

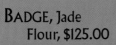

BADGE, White
Salt, $60.00   Flour, $75.00
Pepper, $60.00   Sugar, $75.00
Salt & pepper, $125.00 Set of four, $285.00

BADGE, Jade
Flour, $125.00

Square

BADGE OPEN, White
    Salt, $30.00
    Pepper, $30.00
    Salt & pepper, $65.00
    Flour, $45.00
    Sugar, $45.00
    Set of four, $165.00

BADGE OPEN, Jadite
    Salt, $100.00
    Pepper, $100.00
    Salt & pepper, $215.00
    Flour, $125.00
    Sugar, $125.00
    Set of four, $475.00

BADGE OPEN, Custard
    Flour, $75.00

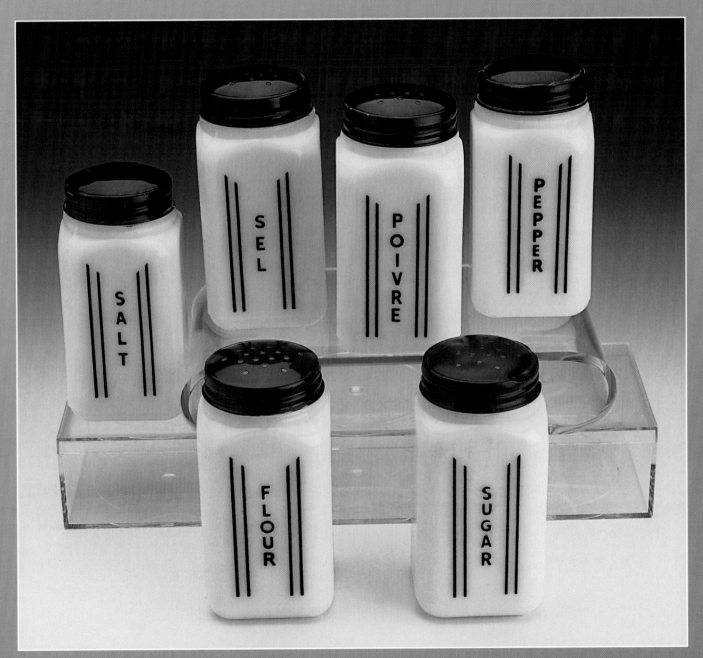

BILINGUAL, Vertical Parallel Lines, French / English, found mostly in Canada

Salt, $60.00	Flour, $75.00
Pepper, $60.00	Sugar, $75.00
Salt & pepper, $125.00	Set of four, $285.00
	Double sided French & English, $110.00 ea.

Square

BLOCK LETTER, Black
Flour, $30.00
Sugar, $30.00

BLOCK LETTER, Custard, two styles
Flour, $45.00
Sugar, $45.00

BLOCK LETTER, Chalaine
Salt, $110.00
Pepper, $110.00
Salt & pepper, $225.00
Flour, $165.00
Sugar, $165.00
Set of four, $575.00
Nutmeg, $225.00

Square

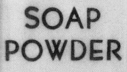

BLOCK LETTER, Jadite Light
  Salt, $75.00
  Pepper, $75.00
  Salt & pepper, $155.00
  Flour, $85.00
  Sugar, $85.00
  Set of four, $335.00
  Nutmeg, $225.00
  Soap powder, $225.00

Block Letter, Jadite Dark
  Salt, $75.00
  Pepper, $75.00
  Salt & pepper, $155.00
  Flour, $85.00
  Sugar, $85.00
  Set of four, $335.00

Square

BLOCK LETTER, Seville Yellow

Salt, $45.00	Flour, $45.00
Pepper, $45.00	Sugar, $45.00
Salt & pepper, $100.00	Set of four, $205.00

Fired-On Green and Yellow Lettered, $30.00 ea.

BLOCK LETTER, White,
Small, 12 oz., pewter tops
    Salt, $55.00
    Pepper, $55.00
    Salt & pepper, $115.00
    Flour, $60.00
    Sugar, $60.00
    Set of four, $245.00

BLOCK LETTER, White, Large, 20 oz., pewter tops
    Salt, $75.00
    Pepper, $75.00
    Salt & pepper, $155.00
    Flour, $75.00
    Sugar, $75.00
    Set of four, $320.00

Square

BLOCK LETTER, White, shown together for size comparison

Large, 20 oz., pewter tops
Salt, $75.00
Pepper, $75.00
Salt & pepper, $155.00
Flour, $75.00
Sugar, $75.00
Set of four, $320.00

Small, 12 oz., pewter tops
Salt, $55.00
Pepper, $55.00
Salt & pepper, $115.00
Flour, $60.00
Sugar, $60.00
Set of four, $245.00

BOX, LARGE, Custard

Salt, $60.00	Set of four, $285.00
Pepper, $60.00	Ginger, $165.00
Salt & pepper, $125.00	Nutmeg, $165.00
Flour, $75.00	Cinnamon, $165.00
Sugar, $75.00	Spice, $165.00

Square

BOX, LARGE, Red Letter
Salt, $100.00
Pepper, $100.00
Salt & pepper, $225.00

BOX, LARGE, White
Salt (not shown), $50.00
Pepper, $50.00
Salt & pepper, $105.00
Flour, $50.00
Sugar, $50.00
Set of four, $210.00

BOX, LARGE, Jadite
  Salt, $70.00
  Pepper, $70.00
  Salt & pepper, $145.00
  Flour, $90.00
  Sugar, $90.00
  Set of four, $335.00

BOX, SMALL, Jadite
  Salt, $65.00
  Pepper, $65.00
  Salt & pepper, $135.00
  Flour, $85.00
  Sugar, $85.00
  Set of four, $315.00

Square

BOX, SMALL, Black

Salt, $60.00   Flour, $75.00
Pepper, $60.00   Sugar, $75.00
Salt & pepper, $125.00   Set of four, $295.00

BOX, SMALL, Delphite
Salt, $225.00
Pepper, $225.00
Salt & pepper, $475.00
Flour, $295.00
Sugar (not shown), $295.00
Set of four, $1,175.00

BOX, SMALL, Custard
Salt, $50.00
Pepper, $50.00
Salt & pepper, $105.00
Flour, $50.00
Sugar, $50.00
Set of four, $210.00

BOX, SMALL, White
Salt, $50.00
Pepper (not shown), $50.00
Salt & pepper, $105.00
Flour, $50.00
Sugar (not shown), $50.00
Set of four, $210.00

Square

EMBOSSED Chalaine Blue, Light or Dark
  Salt, $375.00
  Pepper, $375.00
  Salt & pepper, $775.00
  Flour, $375.00
  Sugar, $375.00
  Set of four, $1,650.00

EMBOSSED Jadite
   Salt, $295.00*
   Pepper, $295.00
   Salt & pepper, $615.00
   Flour, $295.00
   Sugar, $295.00
   Set of four, $1,250.00

   * Add $10.00 for decorated

Square

INITIAL, Caramel
Salt, $65.00

BLOCK LETTER, Caramel
Salt, $50.00
Pepper, $50.00
Salt & pepper, $110.00

GEORGE & MARTHA
$75.00 ea.
$165.00 pr.

Decorated custard, flour $35.00

Hand-painted, $65.00

VERTICAL PARALLEL LINES,
White
    Salt, $30.00
    Pepper, $30.00
    Salt & pepper, $65.00
    Flour, $45.00
    Sugar, $45.00
    Set of four, $165.00

VERTICAL PARALLEL LINES, Black
    Salt (not shown), $225.00
    Pepper, $225.00
    Salt & pepper, $475.00
    Flour, $225.00
    Sugar, $225.00
    Set of four, $975.00

Square

OUTLINED "P"
    Salt, $45.00
    Pepper, $45.00
    Salt & pepper, $90.00
    Flour, $65.00
    Sugar, $65.00
    Set of four, $225.00

STYLIZED CROSS
    Salt, $35.00
    Pepper, $35.00
    Salt & pepper, $75.00

Tipp Novelty Company decorations on McKee or other shakers are located in this section. In most cases where large and small shakers are pictured, the large shakers are McKee and the smaller ones are some other company. All of the small shakers are being identified as Tipp City; however, there are no known manufacturing records to indicate that Tipp Novelty Company made anything other than decorations. For now, we will continue the tradition of calling these small square shakers Tipp City shakers.

ADVERTISING, International Harvester
Salt, $35.00
Pepper, $35.00
Salt & pepper, $75.00

BARNYARD
Cloves, $60.00
Cinnamon, $60.00
Nutmeg, $60.00

Tipp City Decorated

BLACKBIRD

Salt, $70.00	Set of four, $310.00
Pepper, $70.00	Set of five, $495.00
Salt & pepper, $145.00	Grease jar with lid, $165.00
Flour, $75.00	Grease jar without lid, $145.00
Sugar, $75.00	

SONGBIRDS or "BIRDS ON A WIRE"

Salt, $45.00	Flour, $45.00
Pepper, $45.00	Sugar, $45.00
Salt & pepper, $95.00	Set of four, $190.00
Salt & pepper on stand, $115.00	Set of four on stand, $210.00

Chintz ("Climbing Vine") is the actual name for these shakers. This is a typical example of the large decorated shakers being McKee while the smaller shakers are Tipp City decorated, not McKee.

CHINTZ, "Red and Black Vine," McKee, Large
  Salt, $60.00
  Pepper, $60.00
  Salt & pepper, $125.00
  Flour, $65.00
  Sugar, $65.00
  Set of four, $260.00
  Set of four on stand, $280.00

CHINTZ, "Red and Black Vine," Tipp, Small
  Salt, $20.00
  Pepper, $20.00
  Salt & pepper, $45.00
  All others, $35.00 ea.
  Double sided, $40.00 ea.

Tipp City Decorated

CLIMBING VINE, "Posey," Black
Salt, $100.00
Pepper, $100.00
Salt & pepper, $225.00

CLIMBING VINE, "Posey," Custard
Salt, $70.00
Pepper, $70.00
Salt & pepper, $145.00
Flour, $85.00
Sugar, $85.00
Set of four, $225.00

CLIMBING VINE, "Posey," Jadite
Pepper, $325.00

Tipp City Decorated

CLIMBING VINE, "Posey," White
   Salt, $45.00
   Pepper, $45.00
   Salt & pepper, $95.00
   Flour, $55.00
   Sugar, $55.00
   Set of four, $215.00

A PREMIUM DE-LUXE
for any purpose . . .
AT A PRICE YOU CAN AFFORD TO PAY

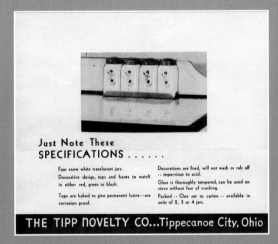

Just Note These
SPECIFICATIONS . . . . . .

Four snow white translucent jars.

Decorative design, tops and bases to match in either red, green or black.

Tops are baked to give permanent lustre -- are corrosion proof.

Decorations are fired, will not wash or rub off -- impervious to acid.

Glass is thoroughly tempered, can be used on stove without fear of cracking.

Packed -- One set to carton -- available in units of 2, 3 or 4 jars.

THE TIPP NOVELTY CO...Tippecanoe City, Ohio

Tipp Novelty Company catalog pages

If you are looking for something unusual in the way of a premium - - something that will appeal to each and every woman, something that has quality appearance, yet low enough in cost for wide distribution, you should investigate this item at once.

Sample and quantity prices on request.

The Tipp Novelty Company
TIPPECANOE CITY - - OHIO, U. S. A.

Extremely PORTABLE . . . .

Jars can be moved without fear of dropping from base. Base is of patented construction, and regardless of angle of tilt jars remain in position. Each jar easily removed.

UTILITY . . . .

Jars contain the essential elements required most often in cooking for flavoring, thickening, etc. Can be used at point of work as entire unit is easily and quickly moved from point to point.

A CONVENIENCE FOR EVERY HOUSEHOLD   DECORATIVE, AS WELL AS USEFUL

Tipp City Decorated

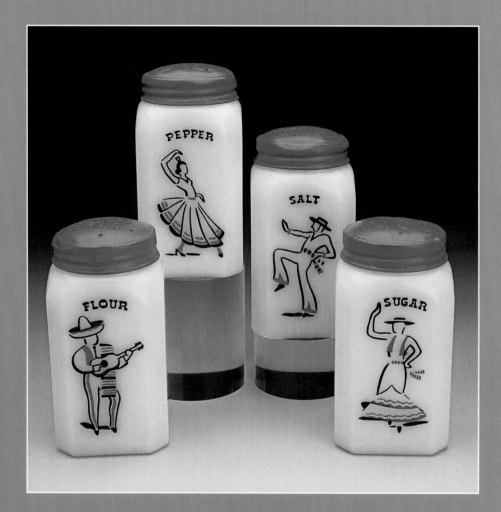

Fiesta
    Salt, $60.00
    Pepper, $60.00
    Salt & pepper, $125.00
    Flour, $75.00
    Sugar, $75.00
    Set of four, $285.00

"Siesta," Red Sombrero
    Salt, $45.00
    Pepper, $45.00
    Salt & pepper, $95.00

FLOWER POT
Salt, $60.00
Pepper, $60.00
Salt & pepper, $125.00
Flour, $65.00
Sugar, $65.00
Set of four, $260.00
Spices, $75.00 ea.

Tipp City Decorated

MAPLE LEAF
Spice, $22.00

NASTURTIUM
Salt, $70.00
Pepper, $70.00
Salt & pepper, $145.00
Flour, $85.00
Sugar, $85.00
Set of four, $325.00

"STICK POTS"
Salt, $60.00
Pepper, $60.00
Salt & pepper, $125.00
Flour, $70.00
Sugar, $70.00
Set of four, $275.00
Spices, $85.00 ea.

Tipp City Decorated

"Tornado Pots"
Salt, $20.00 as shown; $50.00 mint
Pepper, $50.00
Salt & pepper, $125.00 mint
Flour, $65.00
Sugar (not shown), $65.00
Set of four, $275.00 mint

Tulips
Salt, $50.00
Pepper, $50.00
Salt & pepper, $105.00
Flour, $65.00
Sugar, $65.00
Set of four, $240.00
Spices (not shown), $75.00 ea.

"GARDEN GATE," McKee
Salt, $60.00
Pepper, $60.00
Salt & pepper, $125.00
Flour, $75.00
Sugar, $75.00
Set of four, $285.00

"GARDEN GATE," McKee
Salt, design on all four sides, $90.00
Pepper, design on all four sides, $90.00
Salt & pepper, design on all four sides, $185.00

"GARDEN GATE," Tipp
Small shakers, $30.00 ea.
8-pc. set on stand (salt, pepper,
    flour, sugar, cinnamon, paprika,
    nutmeg, and ginger), $265.00

Tipp City Decorated

CHERRIES
    Salt, $70.00
    Pepper, $70.00
    Salt & pepper, $145.00
    Flour, $75.00
    Sugar, $75.00
    Set of four, $220.00

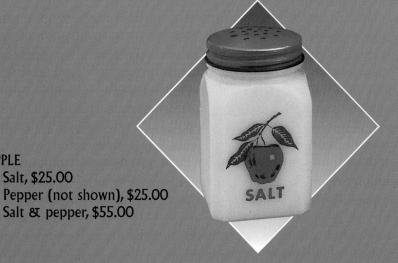

APPLE
    Salt, $25.00
    Pepper (not shown), $25.00
    Salt & pepper, $55.00

FRUIT BASKET (mint with decal)

Salt, $22.00   Set of four, $100.00
Pepper, $22.00   Spices, $22.00 ea.
Salt & pepper, $45.00 Yellow / cracked, $15.00 ea.
Flour, $25.00   Decal mostly missing, $7.00 ea.
Sugar, $25.00

Tipp City Decorated

Scotty versus Scottie has always been a spelling conundrum. Notice that even the original catalog page (on page 126) is inconsistent. Scotty seems to refer to the shakers with three dogs and Scottie to those decorated with only one dog.

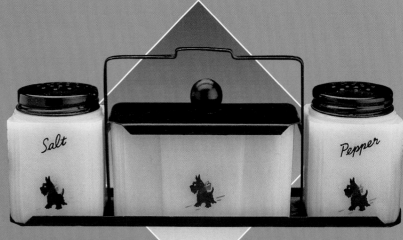

SCOTTIES
Salt, $30.00
Pepper, $30.00
Salt & pepper, $65.00
Grease jar with cover, $165.00
Grease jar without cover, $145.00

SCOTTIES
Flour, tall, $45.00
Sugar, tall, $45.00

SCOTTIES
Spices, short, $45.00 ea.

SCOTTIES
Flour, $40.00
Sugar, $40.00
Spices, short, $45.00 ea.

Tipp City Decorated

THREE SCOTTIES WITH RED BOWTIES, Large
Salt, $70.00
Pepper, $70.00
Salt & pepper, $145.00
Flour, $75.00
Sugar, $75.00
Set of four, $210.00

SCOTTY WITH RED BOWTIE, Small
Salt, $40.00
Pepper, $40.00
Salt & pepper, $85.00
Flour, $40.00
Sugar, $40.00
Set of four, $170.00

SCOTTY WITH RED BOWTIE, Small
Four-sided salt, $60.00
Four-sided pepper, $60.00
Four-sided salt & pepper, $125.00

SCOTTIES WITH RED SWEATERS
Salt, $95.00
Pepper, $95.00
Salt & pepper, $195.00
Grease jar with lid, $165.00
Grease jar without lid, $145.00

WESTIE, Small
Salt, $45.00
Pepper, $45.00
Salt & pepper, $110.00
Flour, $55.00
Sugar, $55.00
Set of four, $225.00

WESTIE, Large
Salt, $75.00
Pepper, $75.00
Salt & pepper, $155.00
Flour, $85.00
Sugar, $85.00
Set of four, $330.00

WESTIE, design on all four sides
Salt, $60.00
Pepper, $60.00
Salt & pepper, $125.00

WESTIE, Red, Sugar, $50.00

Tipp City Decorated

WATERING CAN LADY, Large
Salt, $50.00
Pepper, $50.00
Salt & pepper, $105.00
Flour, $75.00
Sugar, $75.00
Set of four, $265.00
Spices, $75.00 ea.

WATERING CAN LADY, Large
    Salt, $50.00
    Pepper, $50.00
    Salt & pepper, $105.00
    4-pc. set on stand, $395.00
    Grease jar with lid, $175.00
    Grease jar without lid, $155.00

WATERING CAN LADY, Small
    Salt, $45.00
    Pepper, $45.00
    Salt & pepper, $95.00
    Flour, $55.00
    Sugar, $55.00
    Set of four, $215.00

Collectors most often recognize the forest green colored square and ovoid shaped shakers and canisters as being made by Owens-Illinois. This company also manufactured crystal, frosted crystal, and fired colors. Many pieces are marked with an "O" and an "I" within a diamond, as shown here. There are two prevailing designs on the Owens-Illinois square shakers, diagonal lines or squared blocks.

Tea Time

Tea Time Set in Box, $35.00

Bottom view of Tea Time Set

Tea Time Set in Box, $35.00

Accent Shakers

Close-up of Accent directions

Salt, $5.00
Accent, $8.00
Pepper, $5.00
Directions and spoon, $10.00

Hazel-Atlas, $8.00
Owens-Illinois, $5.00
Unknown, $6.00
Owens-Illinois, $5.00
Hazel-Atlas, $8.00

Crystal with Meyercord Decals, 16 oz.
$8.00 – 10.00 ea.

Emerald Green
Salt, $18.00
Pepper with label, $21.00
Flour, $18.00
Sugar, $18.00

Owens-Illinois Glass Company

Block Design

DUTCH, Large, 12 oz.
Salt, $30.00
Pepper, $30.00
Tea, $30.00
Cinnamon, $30.00

DUTCH, Small, 8 oz.
Salt, $25.00
Pepper, $25.00
Salt & pepper, $55.00
Flour, $30.00
Sugar, $30.00
Set of four, $120.00
Nutmeats, $30.00
Cocoa, $30.00
Spice, $30.00
Tea, $30.00

MEXICAN, Large, 12 oz.,
with Meyercord decals, $12.00 ea.

Ruff and Ready "Diagonal Bands"

Crystal
  Salt, $10.00
  Pepper, $10.00
  Salt & pepper, $22.00
  Flour, $12.00
  Sugar, $12.00
  Set of four, $48.00

Crystal Frosted, $10.00 ea.
With label, $12.00

Emerald Green, 16 oz.
  Salt, $18.00
  Pepper, $18.00
  Salt & pepper, $38.00
  Flour, $20.00
  Sugar, $20.00
  Set of four, $80.00

1 DOZ.   16 OZ.

EMERALD GREEN GLASS
PANTRY JARS

OWENS-ILLINOIS GLASS COMPANY
TOLEDO, OHIO

Ovoid and Miscellaneous

Crystal*
  Salt (not shown), $22.00
  Pepper (not shown), $22.00
  Salt & pepper, $45.00
  Flour, $24.00
  Sugar, $24.00
  Set of four, $95.00

Round, Slender, Emerald Green
  $6.00 ea.
  With label, $12.00 ea.

Fired-On Red*

Salt, $15.00	Flour, $15.00
Pepper, $15.00	Sugar, $15.00
Salt & pepper, $32.00	Set of four, $65.00

Emerald Green*
  Salt (not shown), $28.00
  Pepper (not shown), $28.00
  Salt & pepper, $58.00
  Flour, $30.00
  Sugar, $30.00
  Set of four, $120.00

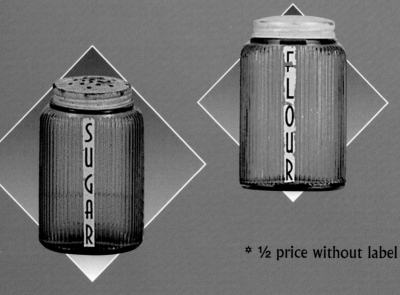

* ½ price without label

Hazel-Atlas and Owens-Illinois shakers are so labeled along with a couple that I have been unable to confirm, but are often "known" in the market as Hazel-Atlas or Owens-Illinois.

Unknown, $6.00
Unknown, $8.00
Hazel-Atlas, $8.00
Owens-Illinois, $8.00
Owens-Illinois, $8.00

Sneath Glass Company

Kitchen cabinets of the 1930s and 1940s often held Sneath Glass products. Most were unmarked and are often referred to as Hoosier shakers. Colored Sneath shakers are rare, but the crystal shakers are abundant. Today, crystal reproductions are available, but their lesser-quality glass is full of bubbles and they come with very thin aluminum lids.

Amber
Without label, $25.00
With label, $30.00

Black, Round
Shakers, $35.00 ea.
Sugar Canister, $165.00

Peacock Blue, $55.00 ea.

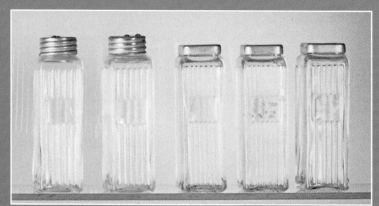

Crystal, $20.00 ea.

Green, Round, "Zipper," $40.00 ea.

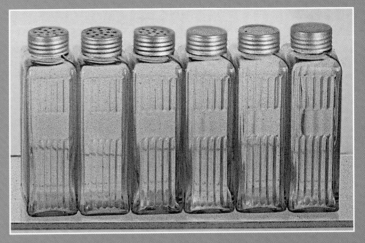

Green, Rectangular, $55.00 ea.

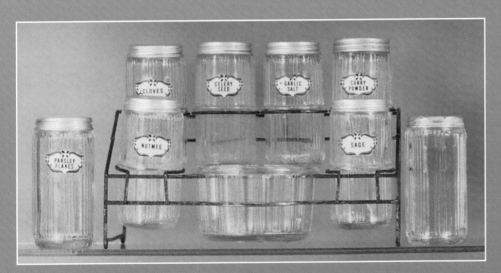

Crystal
Jars, with Meyercord label, $15.00 ea.
Jars, without label, $12.00 ea.
Salt box, $30.00
Set on stand, $175.00

Fired-On Red, $20.00 ea.

Tipp Novelty Company

The catalog pages shown in this section help identify patterns by original names that have not been widely known by collectors. Be sure to read about Tipp Novelty decorations in the McKee section on page 87. The shakers shown in the catalogs are being listed as Tipp City shakers, although it is more likely only the decorations are Tipp. We are following tradition and calling these Tipp City shakers. Tipp shakers may be embossed "Tipp U.S.A." or "Made in U.S.A." on the bottom or, more likely, are unmarked altogether. The unmarked shakers generate a reasonable assumption that someone else made these unmarked versions for Tipp to decorate.

Notice that Salt and Pepper sets with or without grease jars were called Rangette sets in the catalog pages, which could also include a Flour and Sugar. The open grillwork holders were Trellis design, and sets of shakers with spices were called Spicette sets. Spinette sets were those that spun on turntables.

Black Leaf Flower

Salt, $15.00
Pepper, $15.00
Salt & pepper, $35.00
Flour, $18.00
Sugar, $18.00
Set of four, $75.00
Spices, $18.00 ea.
Set of 8 (not shown), $155.00
Set of 12 on stand, $245.00

Black Leaf Flower

Spice Jars, $18.00 ea.

Grease Jars

There were at least two molds for Tipp grease jars, which are shown here together for size comparison. Measurements are provided for each.

Black Leaf FLower, large grease jar with lid, $145.00

Small Rooster grease jar, 4"w x 2³/₁₆"h, $125.00
Large Blackbird grease jar, 4¾"w x 2½"h, $165.00

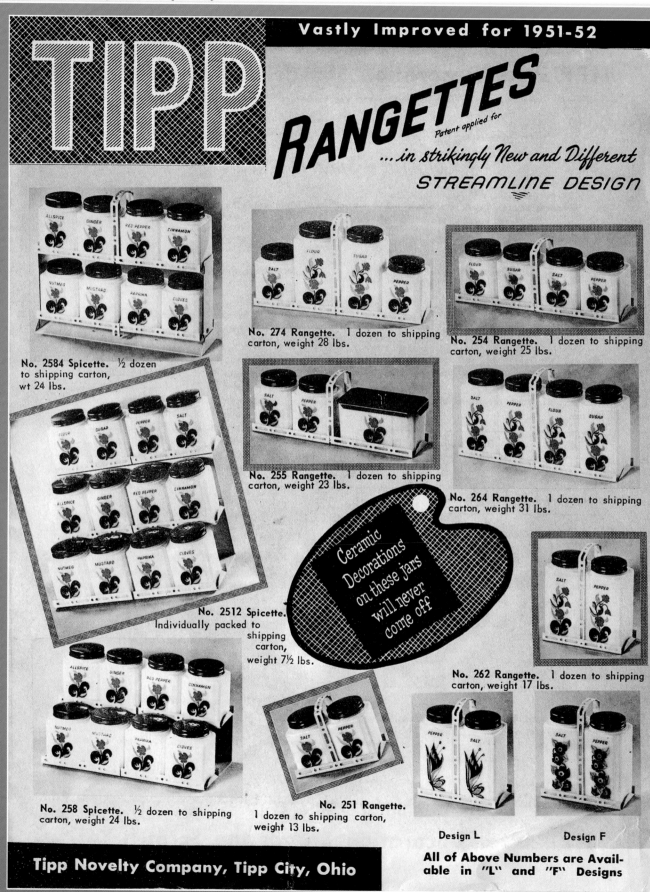

Vastly Improved for 1951-52

TIPP

RANGETTES
Patent applied for

...in strikingly New and Different

STREAMLINE DESIGN

No. 2584 Spicette. ½ dozen to shipping carton, wt 24 lbs.

No. 274 Rangette. 1 dozen to shipping carton, weight 28 lbs.

No. 254 Rangette. 1 dozen to shipping carton, weight 25 lbs.

No. 255 Rangette. 1 dozen to shipping carton, weight 23 lbs.

No. 264 Rangette. 1 dozen to shipping carton, weight 31 lbs.

No. 2512 Spicette. Individually packed to shipping carton, weight 7½ lbs.

Ceramic Decorations on these jars will never come off

No. 262 Rangette. 1 dozen to shipping carton, weight 17 lbs.

No. 258 Spicette. ½ dozen to shipping carton, weight 24 lbs.

No. 251 Rangette. 1 dozen to shipping carton, weight 13 lbs.

Design L

Design F

Tipp Novelty Company, Tipp City, Ohio

All of Above Numbers are Available in "L" and "F" Designs

BASKET, small
Salt, $22.00
Pepper, $22.00
Flour, $22.00
Sugar, $22.00
Spices, $22.00
4-pc. set in box, $165.00
Without box or stand, $110.00

BASKET, large
Salt, $22.00
Pepper, $22.00
Flour, $22.00
Sugar, $22.00
4-pc. set on black or red stand, $110.00
Black stand called "Trellis" by Tipp.

Basket

Catalog photos from Tipp Novelty Company, Tipp City, Ohio, showing how these shakers were marketed.

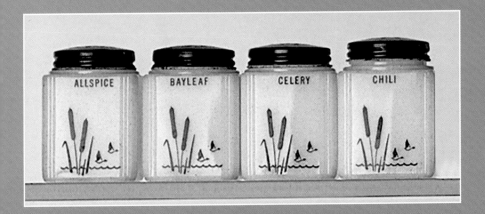

Black, $20.00 ea.
Complete set of 16, $325.00

Cattails

Red, Large, Red Lids
    Salt, $24.00
    Pepper, $24.00
    Salt & pepper, $50.00
    Flour, $24.00
    Sugar, $24.00
    Set of four, $100.00
    Set of four on
        trellis holder, $125.00

Red, Large, Black Lids
    Salt, $24.00
    Pepper, $24.00
    Salt & pepper, $50.00
    Flour, $24.00
    Sugar, $24.00
    Set of four, $100.00
    Set of four on black stand, $125.00

Box Set of Small Red Cattails
    Salt, $20.00
    Pepper, $20.00
    Salt & pepper, $45.00
    Boxed set with stand, $85.00

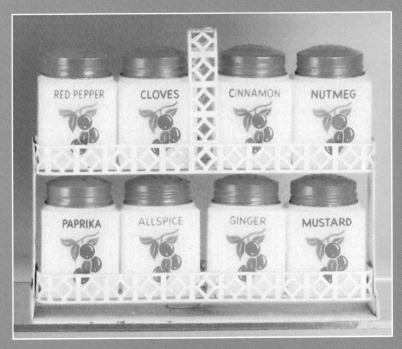

Spices, $24.00 ea.
Set of eight, $200.00
Set of eight on white trellis stand, $225.00

Set of 12 as shown in
Tipp Novelty Company
catalog, $325.00

Cherries

Spices, $24.00 ea.
Set of eight, $200.00
Set of eight on white trellis stand, $225.00

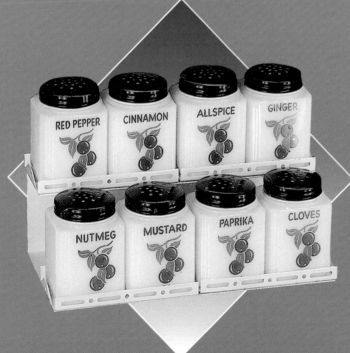

Cherry set as shown in Tipp
Novelty Company catalog

Small
- Salt, $20.00
- Pepper, $18.00
- Salt & pepper, $45.00
- Grease jar with lid, $185.00
- Grease jar without lid, $165.00
- Set as shown on stand, $245.00

Large
- Salt, $22.00
- Pepper, $22.00
- Salt & pepper, $50.00
- Flour, $24.00
- Sugar, $24.00
- Set of four, $110.00

Catalog spinette as shown in Tipp
Novelty Company catalog, $130.00

New "TIPP" RANGETTES
COLORFUL · SMART · PRACTICAL

620-S — SCOTTY
2 doz. to shipping
carton—wgt. 30 lbs.

740-B — BASKET
1 doz. to shipping
carton—wgt. 25 lbs.

520-E — CHINTZ
3 doz. to shipping
carton—wgt. 34 lbs.

No kitchen complete without one or more
of these smart condiment and spice sets.

540-E — CHINTZ
2 doz. to shipping
carton—wgt. 45 lbs.

DECORATIONS — Permanent
—will not wash or wear off as
they are fused into jars at
1050° heat.

SHAKER CAPS — Corrosion
Proof—in bright Polymerin enamel to match—
BASES — of rigid steel. Both
baked at high heat to insure
long *lustrous* life of finish.

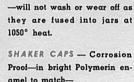

550-S — SCOTTIE
2 doz. to shipping
carton—wgt. 40 lbs.

650-D — DAISY CHAIN
1 doz. to shipping
carton—wgt. 23 lbs.

COLORS — Tops and bases in
RED ★ BLACK ★ BLUE—ROYAL
BLUE — GREEN — YELLOW —
WHITE.

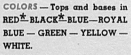

640-B — BASKET
1 doz. to shipping
carton—wgt. 30 lbs.

PACKING — All sets are individually
packed in heavy corrugated cartons. 1, 2,
or 3 dozen to master shipping carton as
shown. Breakage remote when shipped in
standard package.

*ALL STYLES SHOWN AVAILABLE
IN ALL DECORATIONS*

Order by Number and Letter.
Number = style; Letter = decoration.
(Please do not ask us to break standard cartons)
(3rd class freight applies)

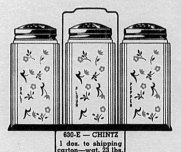

630-E — CHINTZ
1 doz. to shipping
carton—wgt. 23 lbs.

730-D — DAISY CHAIN
1 doz. to shipping
carton—wgt. 19 lbs.

★ RED and BLACK
AS SHOWN

560-B — BASKET
1 doz. to shipping
carton—wgt. 34 lbs.

TIPP NOVELTY CO., TIPP CITY, OHIO

PRINTED IN U.S.A.

Tipp Novelty Company, Tipp City, Ohio

The Chintz ("Climbing Vine") shakers are normally found with red flowers and black vines; note this rarely seen variation of black flowers and red vines. These are Tipp Novelty Company decorated, but the reverse colors may have been a special order for some company or even a special design for someone's fiftieth birthday using black flowers as a joke.

CHINTZ

Top row: Reverse Black Flower
  Salt, $35.00
  Pepper, $35.00
  Salt & pepper, $75.00
  Flour, $45.00
  Sugar, $45.00
  Set of four, $175.00

Bottom row: Red Flower
  Salt, $20.00
  Pepper, $20.00
  Salt & pepper, $45.00
  Flour, $35.00
  Sugar, $35.00
  Set of four, $120.00

New - Colorful - Smart - Practical
"Tipp" Rangettes

Every Kitchen needs one or more of these Smart Shaker Sets

No. 512 Spicette
½ Doz. to Shipping Carton. Wt. 34 lbs.

No. 508 Spicette
1 Doz. to Shipping Carton. Wt. 45 lbs.

No. 550 Rangette
2 Doz. to Shipping Carton. Wt. 40 lbs.

No. 521 Rangette
3 Doz. to Shipping Carton. Wt. 34 lbs.

No. 620 Rangette
2 Doz. to Shipping Carton. Wt. 30 lbs.

No. 540 Rangette
2 Doz. to Shipping Carton. Wt. 45 lbs.

No. 740 Rangette
1 Doz. to Shipping Carton. Wt. 25 lbs.

No. 560 Rangette
No. 506 Spicette
1 Doz. to Shipping Carton. Wt. 34 lbs.

DECORATIONS—Permanent—will not wash or wear off, as they are fused into jars at 1050° heat. Decoration B—Basket, F—Flower, S—Scottie.

SHAKER CAPS—Corrosion Proof—in bright Polymerin enamel to match.

BASES—of rigid steel. Both baked at high heat to insure long lustrous life of finish.

COLORS—Tops and bases in RED — BLACK — BLUE — ROYAL BLUE — — GREEN — YELLOW.

PACKING—All sets are individually packed in heavy corrugated cartons. 1, 2 or 3 dozen to master shipping carton as shown. Breakage remote when shipped in standard package.

All Styles Shown Available in All Decorations

Order by number and letter.
Number—Style
Letter—Decoration

(Please do not ask us to break standard cartons.)

(3rd class freight applies.)

"FLOWER" as designated by Tipp Novelty
Company catalog, POINSETTIA, red
    Salt (not shown), $30.00
    Pepper, $30.00
    Salt & pepper, $65.00
    Spices, $35.00 ea.

Flowers

COSMOS or "Yellow Flower"
12-pc. set, $20.00 ea.
Full set of 12, $265.00
Set of 12 on stand, $295.00
Salt, large, green top, $22.00
Pepper, large, green top, $22.00
Salt & pepper pr., large,
green tops, $45.00

COSMOS or "Yellow Flower"
Salt, $20.00
Pepper, $20.00
Salt & pepper, $45.00
Flour, $20.00
Sugar, $20.00
Set of four, $85.00
Set of four on stand, $105.00

GREEN & ORANGE VINE, four-sided
$30.00 ea.
$65.00 pr.

RED & BLACK FLOWER, four-sided
$25.00 ea.
$55.00 pr.

RED FLOWER
Salt, $25.00
Pepper, $25.00
Salt & pepper, $55.00
Spices, $28.00 ea.

RED & YELLOW FLOWER, Small
Spices, $22.00 ea.
Set of eight, $185.00
Set of eight on trellis stand, mint, $205.00

RED & YELLOW FLOWER, Large
Salt, $24.00
Pepper, $24.00
Salt & pepper on stand, $60.00

131

"TIPP" RANGETTES

Patent applied for

...in strikingly New and Different Trellis Design

No. 151 Rangette. 1 dozen to shipping carton, weight 13 lbs.

No. 154 Rangette. 1 dozen to shipping carton, weight 25 lbs.

No. 155 Rangette. 1 dozen to shipping carton, weight 23 lbs.

...and here's the popular new **TIPP** *SPINETTE* SETS

No. 644 Spinette. 1 dozen to shipping carton, weight 32 lbs.

No. 162 Rangette. 1 dozen to shipping carton, weight 17 lbs.

No. 152 Rangette. 1 dozen to shipping carton, weight 13 lbs.

No. 544 Spinette. 1 dozen to shipping carton, weight 26 lbs.

Decorations on these jars will never come off

No. 164 Rangette. 1 dozen to shipping carton weight 31 lbs.

No. 1584 Spicette. ½ dozen to shipping carton, weight 24 lbs.

No. 163 Rangette. 1 dozen to shipping carton weight 17 lbs.

No. 174 Rangette. 1 dozen to shipping carton, weight 28 lbs.

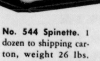

TIPP NOVELTY COMPANY TIPP CITY, OHIO

"Dutch Dancers" and "Produce Basket"

"Dutch Dancers"
Salt, $35.00
Pepper, $35.00
Salt & pepper, $75.00
Flour, $45.00
Sugar, $45.00
Set of four, $120.00

Spices, $45.00 ea.
Set of six, $225.00
Set of six on stand, $250.00

"Produce Basket"
Spices, $25.00 ea.
Set of 12, $325.00
Set of 12 on stand, $365.00

Tipp Novelty Company

Roosters

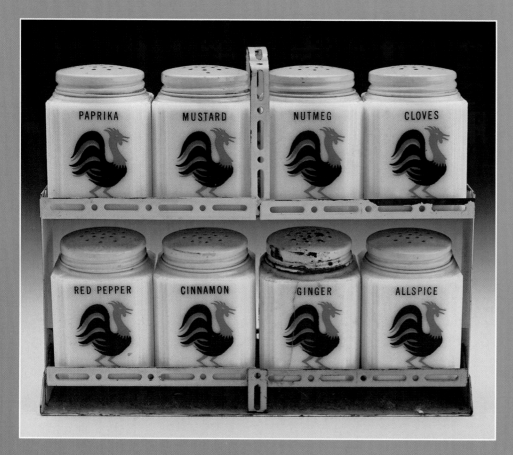

BANNY ROOSTER
Short spices, $18.00 ea.
Set of eight, $150.00
Set of eight on stand, $175.00

ROOSTER
Short spices, $20.00 ea.

ROOSTER, Short
  Spices, $20.00 ea.
  Set of eight, $165.00
  Set of eight on stand, $185.00

ROOSTER, Short
  Salt, $20.00
  Pepper, $20.00
  Salt & pepper in box, $65.00

ROOSTER, Tall
  Salt, $25.00
  Pepper, $25.00
  Salt & pepper, $55.00
  Salt & pepper on stand, $65.00

Roosters

Short shakers, $20.00 ea.
Set of 12, $250.00
Set of 12 on stand, $275.00

Large grease jar with lid, $165.00
Large grease jar without lid, $145.00

Four-sided

Salt, $20.00	Flour, $22.00
Pepper, $20.00	Sugar, $22.00
Salt & Pepper, $45.00	Set of four, $105.00
	Spices, $24.00 ea.

 Flour    *Sugar*    *Salt*    *Pepper*

Original catalog drawing from Tipp Novelty Company

Unidentified

Although some of these appear to be Tipp Novelty Company decorations, we have been unable to discover the manufacturers. Most notable are the shakers with fan-like designs on the sides (see page 147), which are found in crystal and white. There are thousands of Dutch shakers, mostly found in sets of eight, with this side fan design. I see the boy with fishing pole pepper shaker all over Florida, making me suspect it was a premium item in that area.

DUTCH — two views
Salt, $12.00*
Pepper, $12.00
Salt & pepper, $25.00
* With label, add $2.00

DUTCH
$10.00 ea.
Set of three in box, $42.00

DUTCH
$10.00 ea.
Set of eight, $85.00
Set of eight with stand, $105.00

DUTCH
$10.00 ea.
Set of six, $65.00
Set of six with stand, $75.00

Swan
Salt, $20.00
Pepper, $20.00
Salt & pepper, $45.00

Top Hats
Salt, $12.00
Pepper, $12.00
Salt & pepper, $25.00

Niagra Falls
Salt, $20.00
Pepper, $20.00
Salt & pepper, $45.00

Garden Girl
Salt, $20.00
Pepper, $20.00
Salt & pepper, $45.00

Dutch, see page 138

Ships, Green
Salt, $25.00
Pepper, $25.00
Salt & pepper, $55.00

Colonial Bank, $30.00

Ships, Red
Salt (not shown), $12.00
Pepper, $12.00
Salt & pepper, $25.00

White Shakers,
black design
$18.00 ea.

White Shakers
With label, $10.00 ea.
Without label, $4.00 ea.

Musketeers
Spices, $25.00 ea.
Set with paper towel holder, $175.00

Griffiths may be the most prolific shakers found in this book. I have seen these sets on plastic, metal, and wood stands. Sets of eight, 10, 12, 14, 16, and as large as 18 have been spotted. I have only seen white and fired-on brown colors, but others probably exist. Top colors I have seen include black, blue, red, yellow, green, copper, silver, and gold.

Net Weight 3¼ Ozs.

EPICURE SALT

A seasoned table salt delicious on meats, eggs, cheese, soups, and salads. Processed from: Salt, Sugar, Vegetable Protein Derivative, Powdered Onion and Celery Seed, Soya Flour, Spices and Herbs.

THE GRIFFITH LABORATORIES
CHICAGO 9, ILL.

Brown
   With label, $8.00 ea.
   Without label, $7.00 ea.
   16-pc. set, $125.00

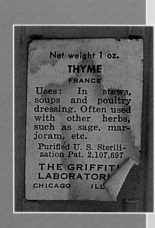

Brown
    With label, $8.00 ea.
    Without label, $7.00 ea.

White, Green Top
    $5.00 ea.
    Set of 16 on stand, $85.00

White, Red Top
    $5.00 ea.
    Set of 18 on stand, hard to find with 18, $110.00

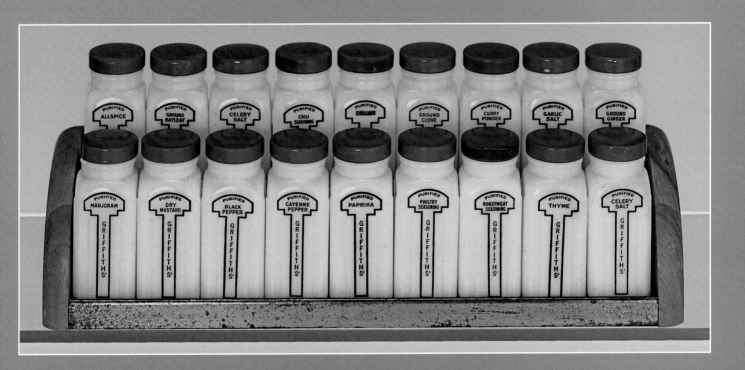

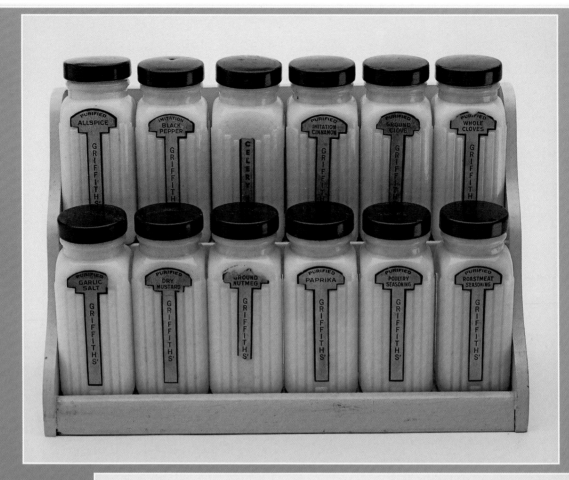

White
    $5.00 ea.
Set of 12 on stand,
    $65.00
Set of 12 on stand
    with labels,
    $85.00

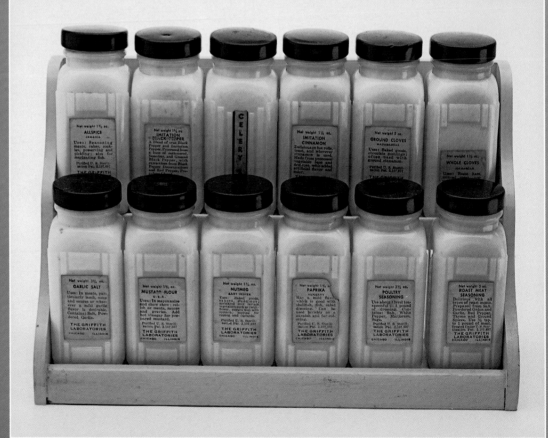

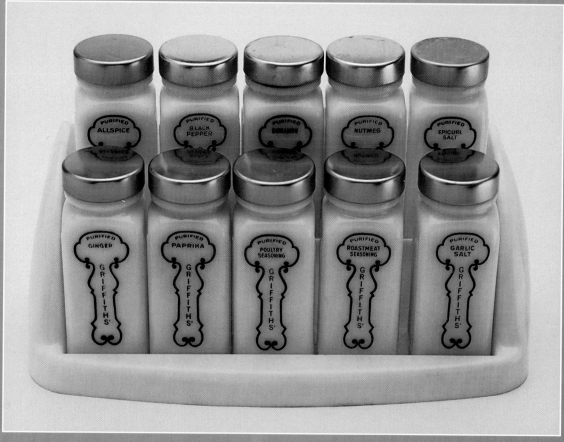

White
With metallic tops, $5.00 ea.
Set of 10 on stand, $55.00

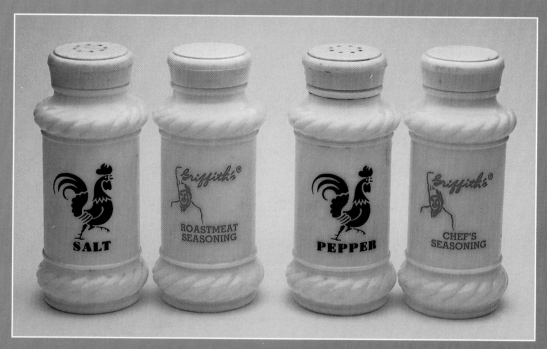

Griffiths with Roosters

Salt, $10.00   Salt & pepper, $22.00
Pepper, $10.00   Roastmeat or chef's seasoning, $12.00

145

Dutch, $10.00 ea.

Embossed "S" & "P"
(Tops have "S" & "P" holes)
 Salt, $12.00
 Pepper, $12.00
 Salt & pepper, $25.00

Magic Chef
 Salt, $25.00
 Pepper, $25.00
 Salt & pepper, $55.00

The Herb Chest, $25.00 ea.

The Spice Chest, $25.00 ea.

Side Fan Design, Reproduction with "Fan-like" shakers

Vintage Side Fan Design, $7.00 ea.

Crystal set of 12 with Meyercord Decals
Small, $10.00 ea.
Large, $12.00 ea.
Set of 12 on stand, $145.00

Decorated Flowers,
$15.00 ea.

Crystal with decals, small, 3⅛", $8.00 ea.

Embossed
Salt, $22.00
Pepper, $22.00
Salt & pepper, $45.00

Clambroth Shakers
Salt, $25.00
Pepper, $25.00
Salt & pepper, $55.00
Sugar, with one-hole top, $45.00

Green, footed ("Tilt-a-spoon"), $325.00
Pink, footed ("Tilt-a-spoon"), $325.00
Green, two shades, Paden City, $185.00
Green, two shades, Paden City, $185.00
Cobalt blue, Paden City, $900.00
Amber, Paden City, $275.00

Amber, Paden City, pinched in, $275.00
Green, Paden City, pinched in, $175.00
Green, Hocking, $175.00
Green, Hocking, $175.00
Green, unknown, $125.00

Green, "Hex Optic," Jeannette, $175.00
Amber, $125.00
Pink, unknown, $175.00
Pink, with red top, Paden City, $240.00
Pink, Paden City "Party Line," $155.00

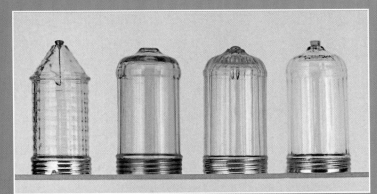

Green, Indiana Glass Co., "Beehive," $220.00
Blue, "Bullet" shape, Indiana Glass #331, $220.00
Green, Paden City, $220.00
Yellow, Paden City, $375.00

Pink, Indiana Glass #331, $295.00
Crystal, Paden City, $55.00
Pink, Paden City, $325.00

Blue, "Monroe Mfg. Co., Elgin, Ill., Pat. Pend." (liquid), $275.00
Pink, "Monroe Mfg. Co., Elgin, Ill., Pat. Pend." (liquid), $200.00
Green, $175.00
Pink, $275.00

Light Jadite, Jeannette, $145.00
Pink decorative, Jeannette, $125.00
Green, Jeannette, $125.00
Yellowish Jadite, Jeannette, $145.00

Pink, Paden City, $125.00
Pink, Paden City, $125.00
Green, Paden City, $120.00
Green, Paden City, $145.00

White "Clambroth," $45.00
Green, $40.00
Pink, $40.00
Orange, $120.00
Forest green, $120.00

Red, $175.00
Amber, horseshoe pattern, $40.00
Green, older style, $40.00
Crystal, marked sugar & cinnamon, $20.00

Ultra-marine, "Bullet," $275.00
Crystal, $55.00
Emerald green, Paden City, $220.00
Green, $175.00

Crystal, Indiana Glass #538, $65.00
Crystal, cone, $45.00

Pink, footed, $275.00
Green, footed, $175.00

Crystal, footed, $25.00
Black, footed, $425.00
Sun-colored amethyst, footed, $65.00
Amber, footed, $275.00

Green, Jeannette, "Hex Optic," #300, $175.00
Pink, Jeannette, "Hex Optic," #300, $225.00
Green, Paden City, "Rena," Line 154, $175.00
Pink, Paden City, "Rena," Line 154, $275.00

Dark jade, Jeannette, $145.00
Pink, Jeannette, $125.00

Pink, Heisey, $220.00
Green, Heisey, $220.00
Crystal, Heisey, $65.00

Pink, measured teaspoon, $275.00
Crystal, $30.00
Fired-on red, $35.00
Blue, $225.00

Crystal, Paden City, "Rena," Line 154,
    individual sugar, $25.00
Amber, individual sugar, $125.00

Forest green, Owens-Illinois, $25.00
Green, $95.00
Green, handled (possibly Pattern Glass syrup), $100.00
Crystal, decorated with flowers, $20.00
Blue, marked "Made in Japan," $15.00

Cobalt blue, $325.00
Green, with green screw-in top,
    Westmoreland, $250.00

Cobalt blue, Paden
City, $950.00

Cobalt blue,
three-footed sugar shaker
(New Martinsville?), $900.00

Green, $275.00
Pink, $275.0

Amber, $150.00

Amber, Paden City, $200.00

KITCHEN GLASSWARE
CRYSTAL — PLAIN AND DECORATED

   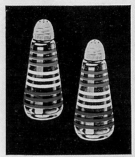

884—5¼" HANDLED BOWL
Pkd. 6 doz.—44 lbs.

800/115—3 PC. KITCHEN SET
Set consists of:
1—884 Handled Bowl
1—793 Salt Shaker—Red Top
1—793 Pepper Shaker—Red Top
Pkd. 72 Sets in 4 cartons—92 lbs.

793—4¼" SALT & PEPPER
SHAKERS—Red Caps
Pkd. 4 doz.—16 lbs.

683—4¼" SALT & PEPPER
SHAKERS
Pkd. 6 doz.—35 lbs.
Display two 683 Shakers with a
247 Jar and Cover (see page 27)
to make attractive Range Set.

586/1776—3⅞" SALT &
PEPPER SHAKERS—Ivory Caps
Pkd. 6 doz.—11 lbs.

586/113—SALT & PEPPER
SHAKERS—Ivory Tops—Floral
Decoration—Pink.
Pkd. 6 doz.—11 lbs.

586/114—SALT & PEPPER
SHAKERS—Ivory Tops—Floral
Decoration—Yellow
Pkd. 6 doz.—11 lbs.

825/8—4⅛" CRYSTAL SALT
& PEPPER SHAKERS—Red
Tops
Pkd. 12 doz.—29 lbs.

825/2—4⅛" CRYSTAL SALT
& PEPPER SHAKERS—Green
Tops
Pkd. 12 doz.—29 lbs.

1830—CRYSTAL SALT &
PEPPER SHAKERS—Alum. Tops
Pkd. 12 doz.—27 lbs.

**ALL ABOVE SHAKERS ARE PACKED ½
SALTS AND ½ PEPPERS TO A CARTON**

151—SALT & PEPPER SHAKERS
Chrome Tops
Pkd. 12 doz.—25 lbs.

793/404—4¼" SALT &
PEPPER SHAKERS—Red with
Ivory Tops
Pkd. 4 doz.—16 lbs.

Kitchen jars and covers are also
available in plain Crystal. The plain
Crystal line includes the 349-1 gal.
jar & cover. This 1 gal. size is not
decorated.

345/4734—½ PINT
KITCHEN JAR & COVER
Pkd. 3 doz.—20 lbs.

346/4734—1 PINT
KITCHEN JAR & COVER
Pkd. 3 doz.—32 lbs.

347/4734—1 QUART
KITCHEN JAR & COVER
Pkd. 1½ doz.—29 lbs.

348/4734—½ GAL.
KITCHEN JAR & COVER
Pkd. 1 doz.—29 lbs.

ANCHOR HOCKING GLASS CORPORATION, LANCASTER, OHIO, U. S. A.   25

1941 *Glassware* catalog, Anchor Hocking Glass Corporation, page 25

Fired-On Anchor Hocking, 4¼", $14.00 ea.; $30.00 pr.

Cobalt blue, possibly bath powder
$22.00 ea.
$45.00 pr.

Tipp City Roosters
Salt, $45.00
Pepper, $45.00
Salt & pepper, $95.00

Raised Dot Design
$12.00 ea.

General Electric Grease Set
Shakers, $10.00 ea.
Grease jar, $50.00
Set, $75.00

These photos will give you an idea of the conditions in which some shakers may be found. Values decrease with poorer condition, as one may expect.

Left to right:
Factory, mint, no wear, no damage
Excellent, very slight wear, no damage or wear
Very good, light wear
Fair, worn, no damage
Poor, leave alone

These are shown only for edification. There is no set percentage for decrease in value. Most collectors will buy first and second condition. Others are bought only if cheap and as fillers until better ones can be found.

Stickney and Poor's Paprika, poor condition, purchased for label identification only.

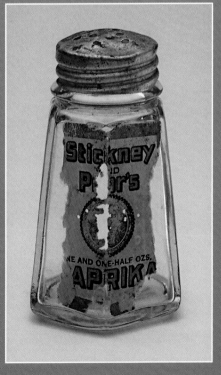

Collectible GLASSWARE from the 40s, 50s, & 60s, 7th Edition

Covering post-Depression era collectible glassware, this is the only book available that deals exclusively with the handmade and mass-produced glassware from the 40s, 50s & 60s. It is completely updated, featuring many original company catalog pages and 19 new patterns — making a total of 121 patterns from Anniversary to Yorktown, with many of the most popular Fire-King patterns in between. Each pattern is alphabetically listed, all known pieces in each pattern are described and priced, and gorgeous color photographs showcase both common and very rare pieces. 2004 values.

Item #6325 • ISBN: 1-57432-351-2 • 8½ x 11 • 256 Pgs. • HB • $19.95

Collector's Encyclopedia of DEPRESSION GLASS, 16th Edition

Since its first edition in 1972, this book has been America's #1 bestselling glass book. This completely revised 16th edition features the previous 133 patterns plus 11 additional patterns, to make this the most complete reference to date. Dealing primarily with the glass made from the 1920s through the end of the 1930s, this beautiful reference book contains stunning color photographs, vintage catalog pages, 2004 values, and a special section on reissues and fakes.

Item #6327 • ISBN: 1-57432-353-9 • 8½ x 11 • 256 Pgs. • HB • $19.95

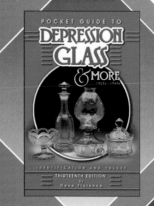

Pocket Guide to DEPRESSION GLASS & More, 13th Edition

Gene Florence

Gene Florence has completely revised his *Pocket Guide to Depression Glass* with over 4,000 values updated to reflect the ever-changing market. Many of the photographs have been reshot to improve the quality and add new finds. There are a total of 119 new photos for this edition, including 29 additional patterns that have not appeared in previous editions. These gorgeous photographs show great detail, and the listings of the patterns and their available pieces make identification simple. There is even a section on re-issues and the numerous fakes flooding the market. This is the perfect book to take with you on your searches through shops and flea markets and is the ideal companion to Florence's comprehensive *Collector's Encyclopedia of Depression Glass.* 2003 values.

Item #6136 • ISBN: 1-57432-309-1 • 5½ x 8½ • 224 Pgs. • PB • $12.95

ELEGANT GLASSWARE of the Depression Era, 10th Edition

This new edition holds hundreds of new photographs, listings, and updated values. This book features the handmade and acid-etched glassware that was sold in department and jewelry stores from the Depression era through the 1950s, not the dimestore and give-away glass known as Depression glass. As always, glassware authority Gene Florence has added many new discoveries, 10 additional patterns, and re-photographed many items from the previous books. Large group settings are included for each of the more than 100 patterns, as well as close-ups to show pattern details. The famous glassmakers presented include Fenton, Cambridge, Heisey, Tiffin, Imperial, Duncan & Miller, U.S. Glass, and Paden City. Florence provides a list of all known pieces, with colors and measurements, along with 2003 values.

Item #6125 • ISBN: 1-57432-298-2 • 8½ x 11 • 240 Pgs. • HB • $24.95

Anchor Hocking's FIRE-KING & More, 2nd Edition

From the 1930s to the 1960s Anchor Hocking Glass Corp. of Lancaster, Ohio, produced an extensive line of glassware called Fire-King. Their lines included not only dinnerware but also a plethora of glass kitchen items — reamers, measuring cups, mixing bowls, mugs, and more. This is the essential collectors' reference to this massive line of glassware. Loaded with hundreds of new full-color photos, vintage catalog pages, company materials, facts, information, and values, this book has everything collectors expect from Gene Florence. 2002 values.

Item #5602 • ISBN: 1-57432-164-1 • 8½ x 11 • 224 Pgs. • HB • $24.95

Florence's Big Book of SALT & PEPPER Shakers

Over 5,000 shakers photographed in full color are featured. Categories include advertising products, animals, chefs, Christmas, decorative, domestic items, ethnic groups, famous characters, gambling, garden items, glass, heads, lamps & lighting, metal, miniature, musical, nodders, Occupied Japan, odd pairs, plastic/celluloid, pottery, religious, risqué, singles, souvenir, sports, steins, transportation, Western themes, wood, and World's Fairs. Famous potteries are represented — Lefton, Holt Howard, Vandor, Shawnee, and more. This book also includes examples of the highly prized Depression glass shakers. 2002 values.

Item #5918 • ISBN: 1-57432-257-5 • 8½ x 11 • 272 Pgs. • PB • $24.95

KITCHEN GLASSWARE of the Depression Years, 6th Edition

This exciting new edition of our bestselling *Kitchen Glassware of the Depression Years* is undeniably the definitive reference on the subject. More than 5,000 items are showcased in beautiful professional color photographs with descriptions and values. Many new finds and exceptionally rare pieces have been added. The highly collectible glass from the Depression era through the 1960s fills its pages, in addition to the ever-popular Fire-King and Pyrex glassware. This comprehensive encyclopedia provides an easy-to-use format, showing items by color, shape, or pattern. The collector will enjoy the pages of glass, from colorful juice reamers, shakers, rare and unusual glass knives, to the mixing bowls and baking dishes we still find in our kitchen cupboards. 2003 values.

Item #5827 • ISBN: 1-57432-220-6 • 8½ x 11 • 272 Pgs. • HB • $24.95

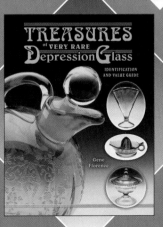

Treasures of VERY RARE DEPRESSION GLASS

Our *Very Rare Glassware of the Depression Years* books were bestsellers for many years, helping collectors spot those rare and valuable pieces of Depression glass that may come around once in a lifetime. This new book features over 1,000 rare or sometimes one-of-a-kind examples of Depression items, as well as elegant and kitchen items. Glass companies featured include Duncan & Miller, Federal, Fostoria, Fenton, A.H. Heisey, Hocking, Imperial, Jeannette, Paden City, Tiffin, and more. Values are given for these rare items, as well as colors, shapes, and sizes. This book is a must for your glassware library. 2003 values.

Item #6241 • ISBN: 1-57432-336-9 • 8½ x 11 • 368 Pgs. • HB • $39.95

Schroeder's ANTIQUES Price Guide

8½" x 11" • 608 pages • $14.95

...is the #1 bestselling antiques & collectibles value guide on the market today, and here's why...

• More than 400 advisors, well-known dealers, and top-notch collectors work together with our editors to bring you accurate information regarding pricing and identification.

• More than 50,000 items in over 500 categories are listed along with hundreds of sharp original photos that illustrate not only the rare and unusual, but the common, popular collectibles as well.

• Each large close-up shot shows important details clearly. Every subject is represented with histories and background information, a feature not found in any of our competitors' publications.

• Our editors keep abreast of newly developing trends, often adding several new categories a year as the need arises.

OUR #1 BEST-SELLER!

Without doubt, you'll find

Schroeder's Antiques Price Guide

the only one to buy for reliable information and values.

If it merits the interest of today's collector, you'll find it in *Schroeder's*. And you can feel confident that the information we publish is up-to-date and accurate. Our advisors thoroughly check each category to spot inconsistencies, listings that may not be entirely reflective of market dealings, and lines too vague to be of merit. Only the best of the lot remains for publication.

COLLECTOR BOOKS
P.O. Box 3009, Paducah, KY 42002–3009
1-800-626-5420
www.collectorbooks.com